THE
DAD TIRED

Q&A MIXTAPE

JERRAD LOPES

HARVEST HOUSE PUBLISHERS
EUGENE, OREGON

Cover design by Bryce Williamson
Cover image © Samorodinov (Cassettes) / gettyimages
Interior design by KUHN Design Group

For bulk, special sales, or ministry purchases, please call 1-800-547-8979.
Email: Customerservice@hhpbooks.com

This logo is a federally registered trademark of the Hawkins Children's LLC. Harvest House Publishers, Inc., is the exclusive licensee of this trademark.

THE DAD TIRED Q&A MIXTAPE
Copyright © 2023 by Jerrad Lopes
Published by Harvest House Publishers
Eugene, Oregon 97408
www.harvesthousepublishers.com

ISBN 978-0-7369-7718-0 (hardcover)
ISBN 978-0-7369-7719-7 (eBook)

Library of Congress Control Number: 2022934016

Printed in Colombia

23 24 25 26 27 28 29 30 31 / NI / 10 9 8 7 6 5 4 3 2 1

To the men of the Dad Tired community
who are stumbling their way toward Jesus
and helping their families do the same

CONTENTS

INTRODUCTION

I remember walking back to my locker, trying to fight back the tears threatening to pour out of my eyes. As a sixteen-year-old sophomore boy in high school, there was almost nothing worse than crying in front of your friends. I stood there with the locker door open, hiding my face and pretending to rummage through my loose papers until I could compose myself before emerging back into the real world again.

My very first girlfriend had just broken up with me, and it was the worst day of my life. I couldn't imagine how I could possibly go on with the rest of my life, let alone make it through the rest of that day.

After what seemed like an eternity, I was jolted out my sulking when my best friend, Chris, gave me a sudden and unexpected slap on the back. It felt more like he was trying to kill a giant spider than give a friend a warm embrace of comfort. I hate unexpectedly being slapped on my back; it's a major pet peeve.

"You okay, man?" he asked.

"Yeah, I'm fine. Why?"

"You don't seem fine. You look like you're about to cry."

Young teenage boys aren't typically the best at reading the emotions in the room, and Chris was putting that reality on full display.

"Shut up, man. I'm fine. Jessica and I just broke up. She was dumb, anyway. I'm fine. Let's just go to class."

I tried to act tough, but I wasn't fine, and Chris knew it.

When the final bell rang for the day, I made my way to the parking lot, eager to get home and process my emotions away from my classmates. As I got closer to my '98 Toyota Tacoma, I couldn't help but notice something out of the ordinary sitting on top of the windshield.

"This mixtape should cheer you up—Chris." Attached to the note was a burned CD (not a cassette tape) with the words "breakup mixtape" written in sloppy permanent marker.

I sat down in the cab of the truck, enjoying a moment of silence and solitude before sliding the CD into the truck's player.

"You'll Think of Me" by Keith Urban started to play through the speakers. I slowly leaned forward and rested my head against the steering wheel, closing my eyes and letting the tears that had been so desperately trying to make an appearance all day finally start to fall.

That mixtape, or more accurately, mix CD, became the soundtrack of my sophomore year. It was the background music from that disc that carried me through the various heartbreaks, celebrations, and confusion of my teenage years. Even to this day, when I hear certain songs from that CD, they bring up emotions tied to those memories.

In many ways, this book is meant to serve you in the same way Chris's mixtape served me back in the day. My hope is that it will act as the soundtrack that carries you along through the many seasons you'll face as a husband, disciple, and father.

To be honest, not every track (a.k.a. chapter) will be totally relevant for the season you may be in. Maybe some tracks will offer you hope in the middle of

Regardless of the current situations you and I find ourselves in, we need to be reminded of the eternal truths found in Scripture.

Q&A MIXTAPE

discouragement, while others may be exactly what you need to hear during a time of celebration, like when welcoming a new baby to the family.

I suggest you skip to the tracks that make the most sense for where you are right now. Something that might not resonate in this season of life may be exactly what you need to hear a few years from now.

I'm not naive; I know you may be in the middle of some really tough things. Pain much deeper than breaking up with your high school sweetheart. You may be experiencing the deep pain that comes with the loss of a child. Or maybe you've found yourself unexpectedly out of work or struggling to provide for your family. The truth is, the older we get, the deeper these wounds seem to cut.

You need more than a mixtape. You need more than some songs that will emotionally carry you through a tough season. You need more than someone's advice that seems relevant today but may not make any practical sense five years from now.

> **Whatever challenge you're currently facing as a dad, you need the truth of the gospel message as your guide.**

You need the gospel. You need Jesus.

Regardless of the current situations you and I find ourselves in, we need to be reminded of the eternal truths found in Scripture.

Whether it's a job loss or a new job. Great health or a devastating diagnosis. A new baby or the loss of a child. Wherever you are, you need Jesus.

I think what meant even more to me than receiving that mixtape back in high school was the fact that my friend Chris was there to walk alongside me in the pain. Listening to songs that could eloquently articulate my hurt in ways that I couldn't possibly verbalize as a sophomore in high school was nice. But it was even nicer to be able to process that hurt with a close friend.

Whatever challenge you're currently facing as a dad, you need the truth of the gospel message as your guide. But I bet you could also use a friend to process that truth with. And honestly, I know how hard it is to find a good friend like that. It's easier to find a guy who will barbecue some burgers and watch a game with you than it is to find a friend who will help point you closer to Jesus.

So here's my encouragement to you: Take a minute right now, and ask God to show you who that friend could be in this particular season of life. Hopefully, someone quickly comes to mind. If so, have the courage to reach out to them and invite them to read this book with you.

If, after spending some time in prayer, no one comes to mind, I would invite you to consider joining our Dad Tired Family Leadership Program. The program is made up of a bunch of guys from around the world who are serious about leading their families well. These men aren't just like-minded friends; they are men who are excited about linking arms with other brothers to chase after what really matters. If you could use some friends like that, we'd love to have you join us. Visit dadtired.com/lead to enroll. Use the promo code MIXTAPE to get a discount.

All right, man. This is me officially handing you *The Dad Tired Q&A Mixtape*. Know that I've spent countless hours in prayer over this and, more specifically, over you. I pray that this little book simply offers the background track to the grand story Jesus is preparing for you and your family.

Excited to jam out with you,
Jerrad

DIAPERS, SLIDES, AND DISCIPLESHIP

What Is Spiritual Leadership?

Today I drove my fourth baby home from the hospital. I don't care how many times you make that drive, it's always nerve-racking. We live about forty-five minutes away from the hospital where she was born, and it took me nearly two hours to get to our house. Turns out, other people don't care about the precious cargo you have onboard and will still relentlessly honk at you as you drive thirty-eight miles per hour down the highway. Even my wife, Leila, looked at me and said, "Babe, I think she'll be fourteen by the time we get home. You can drive a little faster."

I'm called to protect my babies, and I don't care how many middle fingers from angry drivers I might see in the process.

We're dads; that's what we do. We protect.

As I was leaving the hospital this morning, another dad joined me on the elevator down to the parking lot. His wife had just given birth to their first baby the day before, and he was rushing down to get the car ready for their departure. I was standing in the back of the elevator as he hurried to get on

13

before the doors closed behind him. I couldn't help but smile as I watched him.

"Congrats, man. You're probably really excited," I said to him as I watched him fumble his bags. Based on the amount of stuff he was trying to juggle, you would have thought he was leaving on a three-week trip to the desert. He had three massive water jugs in one hand, two suitcases, a diaper bag nearly choking his neck, and a car seat tucked into the crease of his elbow.

"Thanks, man! It's our first!" he said as sweat dripped off his forehead and down into his eyes.

"Can I help you with any of that?"

"No, that's okay. I think I've got it." He settled into a much-needed pause as the elevator doors closed and took us down to the lower level.

"You visiting someone?" he asked after gathering his breath. His eyes were looking down at the box of cookies I was holding in my right hand.

"Oh, no. We just had our fourth. I'm headed down to pick up the car."

"Nice! And…all you have is a box of cookies?"

I sat there in silence for what felt like fifteen minutes.

"Um…I guess I'm just now realizing that this is basically all we brought to the hospital."

We both started laughing like we were old friends sharing an inside joke.

When the elevator reached the bottom, I held the door open so my new dad-friend could make an escape without getting crushed.

"It gets easier; I promise," I shouted as we eventually parted ways in the parking lot.

We both laughed again.

THINGS HAVE CHANGED

As I sat down to write tonight, I started to think about my interaction with that dad on the elevator. It struck me how excited he was and how hard he was trying to be a great dad for his baby from day one. Even in my very brief interaction with him, I got the sense that this was the greatest day of his life, and he was going to do everything in his power to make sure he was the kind of husband and father that his family needed him to be.

I don't think he's alone in that.

I remember right after we had our first child, my grandfather called to congratulate me. He shared a few parenting tips, but it wasn't his advice that stuck out to me during that short call.

"You know what's funny, Jerrad?" he said through a chuckle. "I made it through parenting three kids without changing a single diaper!" It was almost as if he was bragging to one of his old drinking buddies.

For my grandpa, and many others like him, fatherhood meant working hard to put food on the table. That was his standard for what it meant to be the man of the house, and if you did that well, then by every account, you had succeeded as a husband and father.

But I think things have changed.

I live in South Carolina, and I try my best to get outside as often as possible with my kids to enjoy the beauty around us. I'm always struck that whenever we go to a park, you can't help but notice the number of dads playing with their children. Whether it's going down the slides, pushing them on swings, or kicking a ball in the grass; they're everywhere! There is such a sharp contrast from what I remember in my own childhood. Parks used to be the place where only moms would congregate with their kids. Now they are filled with men who are working their tails off to be fully engaged fathers.

> **Something deep in our bones knows that our role as a husband and father is so much more than simply showing up.**

For many of us young dads, we long to do more than just pay the bills and keep a roof over the heads of the ones we love. Our childhoods taught us that our souls need more than food on the table. Our hearts need to be engaged. Our longing for adventure needs direction. Our wandering soul needs a guide to show us the way. Something deep in our bones knows that our role as a husband and father is so much more than simply showing up. And whether we can find the words to articulate it or not, there is something deep within us that drives us to be more than the men who have gone before us. Not that all the men who have gone before us have failed (although some have—majorly) but that we should take the baton that has been placed in our hands and run farther with it.

It's that internal longing that almost instinctively motivates us to go down the slides, wash the dishes, cook a meal, practice ballet, wrestle on the floor, play hide-and-seek, and yes, Grandpa, even change the diapers.

The fact that you're reading these words right now gives me the sense that you know exactly what I'm trying to say. In this very moment, you are doing your best to be a better father and husband. Men who don't care about being a better husband, disciple, and father don't typically read books about it.

And because of that, I want to pause and say something to you that you may not have heard in a while, or maybe even ever.

You're doing a good job, man.

Seriously. Your kids are lucky to have a dad like you.

Maybe your dad was awesome, and you're trying your best to fill his shoes. Or maybe your dad was terrible, and you're committed to being everything he wasn't. Maybe you find yourself somewhere in between. Either way, you're here right now. Reading a book about how to be a better dad. That says a ton about you.

You're doing a good job.

"I'M AN AWESOME DAD"

If you're anything like me, you probably just read that last sentence and let it go in one ear and out the other.

You might be thinking to yourself, *Yeah, that's nice of you to say Jerrad, but you don't really know me.*

I've met dozens of guys who are changing diapers and going down slides but still don't feel qualified to lead their families to Jesus. They find it hard to talk with their kids about the Lord when they are still trying to figure out their own relationships with him. In short, they simply don't feel qualified or equipped to be spiritual leaders in their homes.

A few years back, I was hanging out with a bunch of dads during one of our friend's son's birthday parties. One dad, whom I had never met before, turned to me and said, "So, what do you do for work?"

"Oh, I write books for young dads," I said.

"Nice! I'm an amazing dad!" he said with a giant smile on his face.

I started laughing...until I very quickly realized that he was being serious.

I wasn't quite sure how to recover from that awkward moment and ended up replying with a simple, "Cool."

I was so caught off guard; who says that they're an amazing dad?

I mean, maybe he was an amazing dad. I have no idea. I just had never in my life met a guy who said he thinks he's an amazing father.

Until that moment, I would have said that 100 percent of guys feel like they have room to grow. Now I have to change my make-believe statistic to say approximately 99.99 percent of guys feel like they have room to grow as dads.

Most of us know we have fallen short of what we expected from ourselves as dads, not to mention the standards we know God has for us.

Maybe that's you. Maybe there is a part of you that gives yourself some credit because you know you're trying your best. But that internal voice inside of you keeps telling yourself that you need to be doing better, and if you don't figure it out quickly, you're going to fail your kids miserably.

Let me give you some good news.

You remember Moses from the Old Testament in the Bible? The guy literally murdered someone before God used him to be the spiritual leader of a massive group of people. You want to know the best part of the story? When God calls him to lead his people, Moses begs God to pick someone else. Not because he feels like murdering someone who disqualified him, but because he doesn't feel like he speaks well enough. I think Moses may have been confused about which one of his shortcomings should have disqualified him. Regardless, he was convinced that he was not the right guy for the job (Exodus 2:11-15; 4:10).

Maybe you're not the murdering type like Moses was but more like Jonah, running the opposite direction of where God wants you to go with your family:

> The word of the LORD came to Jonah son of Amittai: "Go to the great city of Nineveh and preach against it, because its wickedness has come up before me."

> But Jonah ran away from the LORD and headed for Tarshish. He went down to Joppa, where he found a ship bound for that port. After paying the fare, he went aboard and sailed for Tarshish to flee from the LORD (Jonah 1:1-3 NIV).

Or what about Abraham, a guy who literally laughed at God when he was told he was going to be used by him in mighty ways:

> Abraham fell facedown; he laughed and said to himself, "Will a son

God has worked with
guys like you before.

Q&A MIXTAPE

be born to a man a hundred years old? Will Sarah bear a child at the age of ninety?" (Genesis 17:17 NIV).

Moses tried to convince God that he wasn't qualified. Jonah ran away from God in his rebellion. Abraham was so convinced that God couldn't use him that he laughed at God. Yet here's what they all had in common: God used each of them in unique and powerful ways.

You might be sitting here today thinking that you have way too many shortcomings to lead your family well. Or maybe you've just been flat-out disobedient; you know what God wants you to do, but you haven't done it. Maybe you're like Abraham and laugh at the idea that God can change the world through you.

Wherever you're at on that spectrum, the reality is that God has worked with guys like you before. This isn't his first rodeo. And if you're willing, he's prepared to use you in mighty ways for his glory too.

Maybe the point isn't about having it all together. Maybe it's more about being willing to go where God sends you. So as we dive into this whole spiritual leadership thing together, I guess I'll just ask you point-blank:

Are you willing to go down whatever path God has for you as a disciple, husband, and father?

If you said yes, you just qualified yourself to be the man God is calling you to be.

Let's go.

QUESTIONS TO CONSIDER

1. When you think about God using you to lead your family, who do you relate to more? Moses, thinking you're too sinful to be used? Or Abraham, thinking there is no way God can do big things with your life? Or Jonah, knowing what God wants you to do but running in the opposite direction?

2. On a scale of one to ten, how would you rank how well you're doing at being the spiritual leader of your home? How would you define spiritual leadership in the context of your own family? What would it look like to improve as the spiritual leader of your household?

3. Are there any men whom you've looked up to as the spiritual leaders of their homes?

INSUFFICIENT FUNDS

How Can I Consistently Invest in My Marriage?

When I was in high school, my friends and I used to have contests to see how much Taco Bell we could eat in one sitting. At lunch during our junior year, we would drive down the street to the fast-food chain and order enough food to feed an entire football team. Not only did we eat more chalupas in one afternoon than a normal person should eat in an entire year, but we would somehow end the day running several miles around the soccer field for practice after school.

I feel sick even as I type this.

Things have definitely changed.

I'm no longer having Taco Bell eating contests with my friends. In fact, if I do happen to sneak in a chalupa from time to time, I make sure to destroy all the evidence like it's a crime scene. I'm embarrassed, not proud of those dietary habits anymore.

That being said, I have to admit that I tried making a run for "the goods" the other day while driving home from a long day of work.

23

It was late, and I had been in back-to-back meetings all day. I knew Leila had already eaten dinner with the kids, and I was craving a fourth meal of my own.

As I pulled into the drive-through, I simultaneously pulled up the hood on my sweatshirt. I didn't want to be seen by the neighbors of my small town (plus, I didn't want to give away all my secrets as to how I'm able to maintain this dad bod figure).

While ordering, I started to have flashbacks of my high school days. *Take it easy, Jerrad. You're not young anymore. Keep it simple*, I said to myself. And I did.

Despite having every desire to order half of the menu, I was disciplined enough to limit myself to one measly combo meal.

"Does everything look correct on your screen, sir?" the teenage Taco Bell worker shouted from his headset.

"Yes," I whispered, trying not to draw the attention of anyone who might be walking by.

"Cool. That'll be seven dollars and sixty-three cents at the first window."

I pulled around to the first window and handed Maddox my card.[1]

He grabbed it without saying a word and turned to his computer to swipe the payment.

He swiped it again. And again. And a fourth time.

"Am I buying Taco Bell for everyone in line today?" I asked through a half-laugh.

"Nah, man. Your card isn't going through."

"Weird. Try it again."

He swiped for the fifth time. "My computer keeps saying your card is declined. Insufficient funds."

---

1. I'll be honest, I have no clue if that was his name.

"Maddox, has anyone ever taught you how to whisper?"[2]

Now, I don't have a lot of money, but I was 99.9 percent sure I had $7.63 in my bank account. But Maddox didn't seem to care about that.

"Sorry, man. You'll have to pull out of line until you can figure out what's going on with your money."

Do you know how embarrassing it is to get money advice from a sixteen-year-old kid from Taco Bell?

I do.

WHEN YOUR MARRIAGE ACCOUNT RUNS LOW

For the record, the chip in my card had malfunctioned, and I ended up having problems at multiple stores that week. But honestly, that wasn't the first time I had to experience the embarrassment of having insufficient funds. There are very few things worse than going through that in public.

My experience at Taco Bell reminded me of an interaction I had with my friend Dan a few years back. We were at church one weekend, and I suggested to him that we try to get together for dinner that coming week.

"Hey, man. Let's grab a bite to eat and watch the playoff game on Thursday," I offered.

"Sounds fun. Let me talk with Sarah and see where my account is at," he said.

I laughed, but he didn't.

"What do you mean?" I asked, now confused.

"Well, taking a night away from the family to have dinner with you will be a withdrawal. I'll have to talk with Sarah about it."

It turns out Dan had plenty of stock in his relational account to spend an evening with me watching the game that week. As we sat together, I couldn't shake thoughts of our previous interaction from the weekend before.

---

2. Okay, I didn't really say that. But seriously, it felt like he was trying to make a town announcement.

"Dude, tell me more about this whole 'relational bank account' you and Sarah have set up," I said as I muted the commercials.

> Too many men try to pull from an account that has run dry.

"Everything we do in our relationships, especially in our marriage, is either a deposit or a withdrawal. Everything you say, the decisions you make, the things you choose to spend your time on...either they are depositing into that relational account or they are pulling from it. Too many men try to pull from an account that has run dry. They are in debt."

That last line hit me. I had been married for over a decade and had never considered that I was constantly depositing or withdrawing in my relationship with Leila.

Dan is a dear friend of mine. We've spent years together trying to figure out what it looks like to follow Jesus and lead our families well. He also gives of his time to serve on our board of directors for Dad Tired (a withdrawal I don't take for granted).

Since our initial conversation about relational deposits and withdrawals, I have not only had the opportunity to learn more about the concept but also been able to watch it play out in real life.

So what do relational deposits and withdrawals look like in a real marriage? Let's take a deeper look.

MAKING RELATIONAL DEPOSITS

Leila and I met in person for the first time at a Chris Tomlin concert.[3] We were introduced online through some mutual friends and had spent a little bit of time exchanging messages, but I was absolutely blown away when

---

3. If there is an award for "Most Christian Way to Meet Your Future Spouse," we would be nominated for sure.

I saw her in person. I was so captivated by her beauty and presence, I don't remember a single moment of that concert (sorry, Chris). I know it sounds cliché, because it is, but it only took one interaction for me to reach the conclusion that I wanted to marry this woman. She captured all my attention and affection from day one.

Over the next several months, I did everything in my power to try to impress her and sweep her off her feet. I think it's safe to say I was way more into her than she was into me at the beginning of our relationship.

At the time, she had only been a Christian for a few years, and I was working full-time at a large church as a worship pastor.

I got this, I thought to myself.

Her love for Jesus was fresh and had a beautiful purity to it. I had been in the church world since I was a young boy and was convinced that I could be everything she wanted in a future husband.

I led worship for thousands on Sunday mornings. I preached the Word. I worked with high school students during the week. I could quote Scripture off the top of my head and had a good Christian answer for every question that she presented.

Man, Leila really hit the jackpot when she found me, I thought.

As a new Christian dating a successful pastor, what more could she want in life? I was convinced our relationship was on a fast-track to marriage, and I couldn't have been happier.

One day we were driving down the freeway, and she was abnormally quiet. I could tell she had been deep in thought, but I didn't know her well enough to know what she was thinking. After what felt like an eternity, she broke the silence with these words:

"Jerrad, are you a Christian because you actually love Jesus or because you get paid to be?"

I felt like I had just been sucker punched in that moment. Where in the world did *that* thought come from? My defenses immediately went up as I felt my heart rate increase and my face start to turn warm.

"I'm not sure what you're asking." I tried to remain calm.

She sat quietly, which made me feel like I had to keep talking.

"Of course I love Jesus. I've been leading people toward Jesus my whole life."

"Yeah, but have you yourself been led to him lately?"

At this point, I couldn't hide my anger. How dare she question my relationship with Jesus!

The rest of that car ride was awkward, to say the least. I dropped her off at her apartment and headed home. As I lay in bed trying to fall asleep, my anger began to subside, and the Holy Spirit started to speak to my soul.

> For the first time in my life, I genuinely asked myself if I really did love Jesus or if I was just playing a part.

For the first time in my life, I genuinely asked myself if I really did love Jesus or if I was just playing a part.

That night, I made a commitment to myself that I was going to be the kind of man that Leila was looking for. I was going to prove to her that I'm a real Christian, beyond the title on my business card.

In the following weeks, I tried to change everything. In the car, I played worship music. When we went out to eat, I prayed before all our meals. I slowed down on the sarcasm and inappropriate jokes that come so naturally to a twenty-two-year-old boy. I was on my absolute best behavior.

And you know what happened?

Nothing. She didn't say a word about it.

And honestly, I was getting exhausted from trying to constantly be on my best behavior.

I didn't feel like I was being myself. I knew that deep down, I was still just acting, playing a role to try to impress a girl. My behavior had changed, but my heart remained the same.

As it turns out, changing your behavior is exhausting.

One night, I was sitting alone in the kitchen of my 500-square-foot studio apartment, and I began to pray. I don't remember thinking that I should start praying. Instead, it was almost as if my soul knew I needed to talk to God and began pouring out to him on my behalf. It reminds me of this verse:

> Likewise the Spirit helps us in our weakness. For we do not know what to pray for as we ought, but the Spirit himself intercedes for us with groanings too deep for words. And he who searches hearts knows what is the mind of the Spirit, because the Spirit intercedes for the saints according to the will of God (Romans 8:26-27).

"God, I'm sorry." Those seemed to be the only words I could repeat, over and over.

As these words came out of my mouth, dozens of past sins started to come to mind. I began to remember events and interactions with great detail. Specific ways I had hurt people, specific words I had said, and specific things I had done in secret.

At this point, my prayers turned into sobs, and I found myself lying facedown on the floor.

I was weeping.

Changing your behavior is exhausting.

I had known for a long time that I was a sinner, but I had never felt the weight of my sin. I knew that I had fallen short of God's standards, but I never took the time to stare those shortcomings in the face long enough to allow the weight of them to penetrate deep into my soul.

It wasn't just that everyone sins; it was that I personally had stepped outside of God's design for humanity and was feeling the pain of it for the first time.

I began to write down all these terrible memories on a piece of paper. My tears were soaking the journal as I wrote. One page turned into three, and three turned into five.

> **I had known for a long time that I was a sinner, but I had never felt the weight of my sin.**

The more I wrote, the harder I cried.

The weight of seeing my sin on paper was nearly overwhelming.

And then, even in my unbearable shame, I felt the Lord speak to my weary soul:

Jerrad, I can forgive and heal this.

I remember thinking, *If my sins can fit onto a few pieces of paper, it's probably not too big for God to fix.*

And just as quickly as the tears and shame had buried me, I was flooded with a deep sense of peace. My body immediately became calm.

I had experienced the grace of Jesus in a way that I had never experienced before. But in order to experience that kind of grace, I had to first feel the heavy weight of my sin.

Amazing grace became truly amazing only after I had fully realized how much I didn't deserve it.

It was that night that I believe I was truly saved.

Yes, I had said "the prayer" a million times before that. Yes, I had been baptized as a child. And yes, I was working in full-time ministry and leading people toward Jesus. But on that night, I truly experienced the kindness of God, which lead me to repentance. That was the night I was saved.

God's kindness is meant to lead you to repentance (Romans 2:4).

Amazing grace became truly amazing only after I had fully realized how much I didn't deserve it.

Q&A MIXTAPE

I woke up the next morning with a different kind of energy. I called Leila first thing in the morning and asked her if we could meet for breakfast. As I shared with her my experience from the night before, I could see her eyes lighting up. She could tell something was different in me. She could see that I wasn't just repeating the words I had learned in Sunday school, but that I had truly encountered the goodness of God.

> The greatest investment you can put into your marriage is to invest in your relationship with Jesus.

We still listened to worship music on our drives, but I sang differently. We still prayed before we ate, but I prayed differently. We still talked about the things of God, but now I was speaking from experience, not from theory.

Here's why I tell you all this: The greatest investment you can put into your marriage is to invest in your relationship with Jesus.

I'm trying so hard not to give you cheesy, churchy platitudes, but any other advice will fall short of the power of the gospel truth. I want to give you practical ways to deposit into your marriage (and I will at the end of this chapter), but I have to plead with you to first invest in your relationship with the Lord.

Here's the truth: If you had the power to become everything your wife desires and needs you to be, you'd already be that guy. If you could do it on your own, you would have done it by this point in your life.

You can't be everything your wife needs you to be without the Holy Spirit changing you from the inside out. And so, if you're asking me what I think you should do to start depositing into your marriage, my answer would be this:

- "Repent therefore, and turn back, that your sins may be blotted out" (Acts 3:19).

- "Put off your old self, which is being cor-
  rupted by its deceitful desires; to be
  made new in the attitude of your minds;
  and to put on the new self, created to be
  like God in true righteousness and holiness" (Ephesians 4:22-24 NIV).

> **You can't be everything your wife needs you to be without the Holy Spirit changing you from the inside out.**

You can't fake righteousness and holiness,
man. At least not for long. It's too exhausting.
You need Christ to change you in ways that you
are unable to change yourself.

You want to love your wife really well? Love Jesus more than anything
else. Face your sins head-on, feel the weight of them, and then let the kindness of God lead you to repentance.

It's the greatest deposit you will ever make.

SAY NO TO ALMOST EVERYTHING

Men who are being transformed by the renewing of their minds (Romans
12:2) start to become laser-focused on what God is calling them to. As God
begins to rid you of your old ways, you begin to find clarity on where you
are trying to go.

> Therefore, since we are surrounded by so great a cloud of witnesses,
> let us also lay aside every weight, and sin which clings so closely, and
> let us run with endurance the race that is set before us, looking to
> Jesus, the founder and perfecter of our faith, who for the joy that was
> set before him endured the cross, despising the shame, and is seated
> at the right hand of the throne of God (Hebrews 12:1-2).

So, what is "the race that is set before us"?

Well, if you are a man who is trying to follow Jesus, the race is clear. We are to be disciples who look, sound, and act a whole lot like Jesus. We are to be husbands who love and pursue our wives with the same kind of love and pursuit with which Jesus chases us down. And we are to be fathers who intentionally lead and raise our children to be Jesus-loving disciples, sent out into the world for his glory.

You can't fake righteousness and holiness, man.

That's the "finish line" of the race for me. Whether the race ends tomorrow or eighty years from now, I want to be able to run with endurance toward that goal.

I imagine if you're reading this, you probably have very similar goals. So it begs the question, What am I running toward that isn't accomplishing that goal? In other words, where am I taking out unnecessary withdrawals?

I'll be honest—I really want a boat.

The other day my best friend said to me, "You know what B.O.A.T. stands for, don't you, Jerrad?"

"No," I said, falling right into his trap.

"Bust Out Another Thousand." He started laughing. "Don't get a boat, man. Those things are money pits that end up sitting in your driveway collecting rust."

He's probably right. I've heard the same advice 1,000 times in 1,000 different ways.

But I'm stubborn. I tend to only learn lessons from making my own mistakes.

And so, I continue to have an envelope in my sock drawer titled "Jerrad's Boat Fund." Every time I officiate a wedding or sell something from my garage on Facebook Marketplace, I stuff the cash into that envelope. Every extra dollar I make goes toward the goal of buying myself a little aluminum fishing boat.

The other day, the faucet on our kitchen sink broke. After hours of watching YouTube videos and trying to fix the dumb thing on my own, I had to come to grips with the fact that I simply would be forced to buy a new one. It caused me a great deal of pain to pull some cash out of my boat fund and drive down to Home Depot to purchase a new faucet.

"Are you sure we need a kitchen faucet?" I whined to Leila.

"Yes, Jerrad. We absolutely need a kitchen faucet more than we need a boat."

I disagreed, but she still seemed to have won that argument.

Here's the point: Every time you make a withdrawal, you are moving away from your goal. And if you make too many unnecessary withdrawals, eventually you'll find that your account has run empty.

It might be helpful to ask yourself right now, *What's the balance of my relational account with my wife?*

When was the last time you made a deposit into that account? What was the last withdrawal?

Sometimes withdrawals are necessary, like when you need a new kitchen faucet. You may be asked to put in overtime on a project that needs to get done at work. Or maybe a family member falls seriously ill, and you need to spend more time with them than you normally would. These are all necessary withdrawals, but remember, they are withdrawals nonetheless.

Some withdrawals, however, are completely unnecessary and can be fully avoided. Like when I take money out of my boat fund to buy two packs of Oreos at the grocery store. Or when I went to get the oil changed in our minivan and came back with a puppy.

An unnecessary withdrawal in your marriage might look like watching another game with the guys when your wife could use a date night. Or spending money on a new toy or hobby when your wife asked you to save money. It might look like spending too much time on work, or sports, or video games, or whatever seems to be capturing your attention these days.

These withdrawals may seem small and without consequences, but spending a dollar here and a dollar there may lead to you one day going to make a purchase and having nothing left in your account.

I can't tell you the amount of DMs I've received from guys on Instagram (@dad.tired) telling me that their wife left them or brought up divorce completely out of the blue.

"I seriously didn't see this coming." I've heard that on multiple occasions over the years.

I know everyone's story is unique, but for the most part, my guess would be that these men had spent their marriages making small withdrawals without ever realizing that their account was getting dangerously low.

Brother, your wife may not up and leave you out of the blue, but I can assure you that some guys don't have a clue as to how dangerously low their marriage account balance is.

Don't wait until you get declined for having "insufficient funds" before you do something about it.

Say no to almost everything.

Seriously.

When your friends ask you to hang out again, it may be time to say no. When your boss asks you to take on that extra project, maybe say no. When everything inside of you is screaming to "veg out" and watch TV all day, say no.

Saying yes and taking out a withdrawal takes you one step away from reaching your goal.

May we be men who repent of our sins, who seek Jesus with every ounce of our being. Men who boldly ask God to show us where we need to grow and then allow his Holy Spirit to transform us. Men who don't live busy lives and say yes to everything, but instead say yes to the things that matter. May we be men who are not rich with earthly treasure but can hold our heads high, knowing our relational accounts are abundantly full and never at risk of running empty.

> **May we be men who repent of our sins, who seek Jesus with every ounce of our being.**

TEN DATE-NIGHT DEPOSIT IDEAS

Finding time to date my wife became a lot harder after having a kid. Add three more kids to the mix, and it can feel nearly impossible. Fortunately, we have some grandmas in our life who love to watch our children, but I know that isn't the reality for everyone. I've heard of some couples who do monthly date-night trades with their friends. This might look like you watching your friends' kids once a month so they can go on a date, and then they do the same for you on another day of the month. We've utilized this in the past, and it was a huge win for both couples (and the kids get to have playdates with their friends twice a month).

Another option would be to hire a babysitter once a month. I know this can add up quickly, so you may need to look at your budget and reflect on actual financial withdrawals that aren't getting you closer to your eternal goals. Dating your wife may require you to sacrifice the video streaming service, the extra lattes, or some other unnecessary goodies each month.

As a rule of thumb, Leila and I try to block off date nights on our anniversary date of each month. Our wedding anniversary is January 30, so we block off and protect the thirtieth of each month to connect with each other on a date.[4]

Dating your spouse doesn't have to be extravagant or expensive. But it does have to be intentional. Here are ten cheap ways you can make a date-night deposit:

1. Go to the library or used bookstore and search for one book that would interest your spouse.

2. Go on a long walk around the neighborhood, regardless of the weather. The crazier the weather, the more fun it will be. (Leila and I once went on a long walk in the middle of a storm and laughed our heads off as our umbrella completely broke apart and flew out of my hands.)

3. Go to a local theater performance put on by the city or local high school.

4. Go garage sale hunting. Give yourself ten dollars to find the funniest or most clever gift for your spouse.

5. Learn a new board game together.

6. Walk around your local pet store (without making an impulsive financial withdrawal!).

7. Bake a wedding cake together and then look through your wedding album as you eat it.

---

4. When we had only two children, we tried to date weekly. This just isn't the reality anymore. So now we work to have one date out of the house each month, while trying to find intentional ways to connect daily or weekly at home (usually over a cup of coffee).

8. Take a class to learn something new to both of you (such as art, cooking, or dance).

9. Find a nearby arcade and see how many tickets you can collect.

10. Put the kids to bed, pop some popcorn, light some candles, and find a show that you both used to watch as kids.

QUESTIONS TO CONSIDER

1. What are some consistent relational deposits in your marriage?

2. What are things that cause relational withdrawals in your marriage?

3. What are you currently saying yes to each week or each month that you could start saying no to?

GOLDFISH AND MEXICAN FOOD

How Can I Maintain Intimacy with My Wife?

My kids have been asking me to buy them a pet since they could talk. I'm probably a terrible dad, but I'm just convinced we aren't a pet family. I've been known to kill our fake plants from IKEA; how in the world am I going to care for a living animal in our home?

The other day they launched a full-fledged campaign. They must have had some meeting in their room the night before, because they woke up motivated with a vengeance.

"Dad, pleeeeease, can we get a puppy? I promise we'll feed it, take it on walks, and pick up all its poop in the yard! We'll never ask for anything ever again."

I chuckled at that last line. Oh, if I had a nickel for every time I've heard those words come out of their little mouths.

"Absolutely not," I said in my stern dad voice.

"Please, Dad! Don't you love us and want us to be happy?"

Seriously, where do they learn these barbaric tactics?

"Okay. I'll make you a deal. I will buy you a goldfish. If you can keep that goldfish alive for a year, we'll talk about upgrading to a mammal."

Cheers erupted in the living room. They were literally dancing around the house in celebration.

Little did they know, they may have won the battle, but I would ultimately win the war. A goldfish would only set me back about three bucks, and I knew there was no way they could keep that thing alive.

"Load up. Let's go to the pet store."

I grabbed my keys and made my way to the car.

Before the garage door could close behind me, I heard a voice in the distance: "Wait! Don't you think you should think this through a little bit, babe?" my wife yelled from the other room.

"What's that?" I yelled back.

She came into the garage so she could look me in the eyes.

"Don't you think we should give this some more thought? I mean, like, have a plan?"

"A *plan?*" I asked. "It's a goldfish. My plan is to spend three dollars on a plastic bowl and a fish that will be dead by the end of the week. I'll be home in twenty minutes."

"I don't think this is a good idea," she said as I packed the kids into the car and headed toward the nearest pet store.

We arrived at the store and quickly loaded our cart with a small bowl, four goldfish (they each wanted their own), and a small bottle of fish flake food.

"All right, let's get out of here," I said to my giddy squad as we made our way to the checkout line.

"You know you're going to kill those fish, right?"

I turned around to find the voice that I was hearing: "Huh? Who said that?"

My kids looked at me, confused.

"You're going to kill those fish," I heard again as a woman named Linda came out from behind the lizard cage. She was about half my height and twice my age, with small pieces of what looked like bark dust or possibly bird food stuck in her hair.

"If you're planning on killing those fish, then you have everything you need in your cart. Otherwise, you're going to need a lot more than that."

Oh boy. I did not plan to run into the president of the PETA volunteers' association during my mission.

"Oh. I figured they'd just need some food and water, since they're just goldfish," I said with a big smile, trying to diffuse her apparent frustration with me.

"Absolutely not. Fish need a lot more than that to be happy."

I kid you not, Linda spent the next forty-five minutes walking my children around that dumb store while loading up my cart. By the time we were ready to check out, she had swapped the goldfish out with colorful betta fish and replaced my small plastic bowl with some high-end, state-of-the-art fish tank that looked like it needed its own room. My cart now contained a water temperature regulator, organic food, water filters, fake plants, and a sunken pirate ship for decoration.

"That'll be $177.29," she said, now smiling as she took my credit card.

I had just been robbed by a little old lady who feeds lizards for a living.

My kids were on cloud nine, but I knew Leila was going to kill me when we arrived home.

Maybe I should have had a plan.

INTIMACY IS LIKE A BETTA FISH, NOT A GOLDFISH

I spend my days talking with the guys in our Dad Tired community about what it looks like to be the spiritual leaders of their homes.[1] Without fail, I end up hearing some version of this: "My wife and I just aren't as intimate as I wish we were." This is one of the most common phrases I come across.

I think if they were being honest, though, most of those guys would admit they really mean, "I wish we had more sex."

For many of us guys, we often use the words "intimacy" and "sex" interchangeably. Although sex is most definitely part of intimacy, it's also so much more. The truth is, I believe many of us men go into marriage the same way I went into the pet store that day, thinking, *I just need a bowl, a fish, and some fish flakes, and we'll be good.*

> Satan has a long track record of taking what is true and then twisting it slightly to cause hurt and confusion.

Or in the case of marriage, *We just need to eat, sleep, work, have sex, and pay our bills, and we should be good.*

If you've been married longer than six weeks, you've likely come to realize that intimacy within the context of marriage is so much more complex than that.

And honestly, that shouldn't surprise us.

If it's true that we are the image-bearers of God, shouldn't we be more complex than goldfish in order to accurately reflect our Creator?

So if you'd be so kind to allow me, I'd like to be your "Linda" for the day and fill your cart with some of the tools needed to help grow and maintain intimacy within a healthy marriage.

---

1. "Home," Dad Tired, connect.dadtired.com.

INTIMACY ON EVERY LEVEL

Satan has a long track record of taking what is true and then twisting it slightly to cause hurt and confusion. Look at Genesis 3:1-5, for example:

> Now the serpent was more crafty than any other beast of the field that the Lord God had made.
>
> He said to the woman, "Did God actually say, 'You shall not eat of any tree in the garden'?" And the woman said to the serpent, "We may eat of the fruit of the trees in the garden, but God said, 'You shall not eat of the fruit of the tree that is in the midst of the garden, neither shall you touch it, lest you die.'" But the serpent said to the woman, "You will not surely die. For God knows that when you eat of it your eyes will be opened, and you will be like God, knowing good and evil."

You see what's happening here? God said you can't eat from *one* particular tree. Satan said you can't eat from *any* tree.

Satan's lies always have a hint of truth to them.

Here's a lie he may be whispering into your ear: "If we had more sex, we'd have a better marriage."

Now, be careful, because some of that is true. Sex is beautiful and most definitely can lead to more intimacy within a marriage. But it's not all true (as is always the case when the evil one speaks).

> **Satan's lies always have a hint of truth to them.**

Let me say it another way: Great sex within a marriage does not always lead to intimacy. There are many couples who have a wonderful sexual connection and yet couldn't be further apart.

The truth? Sex is a beautiful and necessary component of marriage. The lie? Sex alone will bring the intimacy God has planned for you and your spouse.

You're not goldfish. Your souls need more.

FOUR COMPONENTS OF INTIMACY

Throughout the Scriptures, we see God referring to himself as the groom and his people as his bride. It happens so often, in fact, that it feels like God is really trying to make a very specific point. Check out these verses:

- "I will make you my wife forever, showing you righteousness and justice, unfailing love and compassion. I will be faithful to you and make you mine, and you will finally know me as the LORD" (Hosea 2:19-20 NLT).

- "Husbands, love your wives, as Christ loved the church and gave himself up for her" (Ephesians 5:25).

- "I saw the holy city, new Jerusalem, coming down out of heaven from God, prepared as a bride adorned for her husband" (Revelation 21:2).

Read the Scriptures long enough, and it will become obvious that God is using the marriage relationship to paint a picture of what his relationship is like with the church. So it makes sense that whenever we are trying to figure out what it looks like to love our wives well, we must first look at the relationship between God and his people.

Take a look at how God (the groom) tells us (his bride) to love him: "You shall love the Lord your God with all your heart and with all your soul and with all your strength and with all your mind, and your neighbor as yourself" (Luke 10:27).

Whenever we are trying to figure out what it looks like to love our wives well, we must first look at the relationship between God and his people.

Apparently love within this relationship is a little more like a betta fish and a little less like a goldfish. Which, again, makes sense, right?

God didn't create stars in his image. He didn't create mountains in his image. He didn't create horses, fish, or monkeys in his image. Only humans were created in his image.

> Then God said, "Let us make man in our image, after our likeness. And let them have dominion over the fish of the sea and over the birds of the heavens and over the livestock and over all the earth and over every creeping thing that creeps on the earth."
>
> So God created man in his own image, in the image of God he created him; male and female he created them. And God blessed them. And God said to them, "Be fruitful and multiply and fill the earth and subdue it, and have dominion over the fish of the sea and over the birds of the heavens and over every living thing that moves on the earth" (Genesis 1:26-28).

This means that you and your wife hold within you the likeness of God himself. You are created to be complex and able to love in a multitude of ways because your maker is the author of complexity and the embodiment of love itself. A fish cannot love with all of its heart, soul, mind, and strength because it was not created in the image of God. It doesn't possess the ability to love like that.

> **You and your wife hold within you the likeness of God himself.**

But you do.

In fact, you must.

You have been commanded to love God with every part of who you are, just as God loves you with every part of who he is.

So what does it look like to love your wife the way God is loving you?

More specifically, what would it look like to love your wife with all your heart, mind, soul, and strength?

Emotional Intimacy: Loving Your Wife with Your Heart

I'll be honest with you—Leila spent the first few years of our marriage feeling like she was walking on eggshells around me. And for good reason. I thought I had the world figured out as a young twentysomething, but I was incredibly emotionally immature. When we would get into a fight, I didn't know how to talk it out in any healthy or productive ways. My immaturity, combined with not having a dad around to teach me this stuff when I was a kid, led to me having no effective tools to use in marriage. Simple disagreements would turn into me not talking to her for days.

> You have been commanded to love God with every part of who you are, just as God loves you with every part of who he is.

The bottom line was that my wife didn't feel emotionally safe with me. And a lack of emotional safety will always lead to a lack of emotional intimacy.

Ask yourself, Does your wife feel like you are an emotionally safe place for her to land? Of course you would lay down your life for her, but do you work just as hard to protect her heart and emotions? This is where true intimacy begins: when two people feel completely safe around each other.

In our journeys of becoming the men God has called us to be for our families, we must first learn how to provide emotionally safe environments in our homes. Here are some questions I try to ask myself regularly to evaluate how I'm doing in this area. I pray that they're helpful to you as well.

- When was the last time I asked my wife how she was doing and then gave her the time and space to share what was going on in her heart?

- How well am I listening to my wife on a daily basis? Am I her go-to person to share what's on her mind, or does she feel like she must go to friends, family, or social media in order to be truly heard?

- When she tells me things that are hard for me to hear, how do I respond? Am I willing to truly listen to how she is feeling, or do I feel the need to be defensive, loud, or purposely silent?

One of the most beautiful and unimaginable qualities of God is that he knows all of who we are—and he still loves us fully.

> O Lord, you have searched me and known me! You know when I sit down and when I rise up; you discern my thoughts from afar. You search out my path and my lying down and are acquainted with all my ways. Even before a word is on my tongue, behold, O Lord, you know it altogether (Psalm 139:1-4).

Listen, if you knew me to that level, you probably wouldn't even read this book. I'm a broken and messed-up man. But God knows all of me and continues to love me fully.

In turn, I trust him completely. He is a safe and soft place for me to land. His knowing all of me and loving all of me build trust and intimacy. This is how we love our brides the way God loves his.

Intimacy doesn't start in the bedroom; it starts when your wife feels truly safe.

Friend, intimacy doesn't start in the bedroom; it starts when your wife feels truly safe. It starts when she believes to the depths of her being that you want to know all of who she is and will love all of her—when she can trust that you are after the depths of her heart and will respond with emotional maturity when she lets you into those sacred places.

Want more intimacy with your wife? Start there.

Intellectual Intimacy: Loving Your Wife with Your Mind

Leila is smarter than me.[2]

Honestly, I wasn't sure that was even true, so at our last family meeting[3] I asked the kids, "Who is smarter, me or Momm—"

"MOMMY!" they shouted in unison before I could even finish the question.

Deep down, I knew it was true. I guess I was just hoping it wasn't so obvious.

Leila really is smarter than me. If you spend more than ten minutes with us together in the same room, you'll start to question how I even convinced her to marry me.

She has a bachelor of science degree in nursing. She's been trained in medical specialties I can't even pronounce. Me, on the other hand...I barely made it through high school.

Sometimes she'll come home from work and tell me about her day. I try as hard as I can to keep my facial expressions from revealing that I have absolutely no idea what she's talking about.

And yet even though she is worlds ahead of me when it comes to intellect, I can say with confidence that we share a deep intellectual intimacy. Not because I'm taking online classes or trying harder to read more books, but because I've committed to asking her questions about what she is most passionate about.

---

2. It took me about twenty-six minutes to have enough courage to type those words.

3. Okay, I'll slow down on the footnotes, but you can grab a copy of our Family Meeting Journal at dadtired.com/familymeeting.

Intellectual intimacy happens when two people are willing to explore the depths of what is happening in each other's minds.

If you were to turn on the most popular sitcoms in the past twenty years, you'd likely find one of the main characters to be a clueless husband or father. This is what our culture has reduced men to: a bunch of hollow-brained thinkers who simply go to work and try not to get in the way of what the woman is doing at home.

Friends, this isn't who you are.

The fact that you're reading this book right now, trying to learn what it means to be an engaged spiritual leader of your home, proves your depth.

> **You have what it takes to connect on an intellectual level with your wife.**

God has given you a sharp mind to think, lead, and problem solve. You can have deep, intellectual conversations that allow you to connect in powerful ways with your spouse.

And I can promise you, your wife longs for that.

You don't need to have all the answers to have intellectual intimacy, but you do need to be curious. And again, the fact that you're reading this book already shows that you're a curious person. Channel that curiosity toward your wife, and then things that she's passionate about, and you will begin to connect at a deeper level.

The smartest people I know don't have all the answers; they simply have really good questions.

The next time you're with your wife, give her the space to share something deeply with you, and then practice asking good follow-up questions like these:

- What do you like about that?

- How does that make you feel?

- Why do you think you feel that way?

Don't sell yourself short—you have what it takes to connect on an intellectual level with your wife. Take your bride on a date this week. Skip the conversation about busy schedules, messy houses, and chore charts, and instead, dive into the depths of what is deep on her mind.

Spiritual Intimacy: Loving Your Wife with Your Soul

Seven years ago, I thought my marriage was going to end in a divorce. We had been married less than five years and already had two young kids together. I was coming off a failed church plant and found myself deeply hurt by the church and its leaders. I was ready to give up on ministry altogether and almost ready to give up on my family.

I was depressed and pulled away from my wife and my children. I was in a dark hole spiritually, emotionally, and relationally.

As devastating as this reality was for me, it wasn't new for my family legacy. Every man in my family eventually bailed on his wife and kids. My dad left when I was three. My uncles left my aunts. My grandpas divorced my grandmas. This was the reputation of the men in my family, and it was going to soon be my reputation as well.

But God has a different reputation than mine and had a different plan for my life.

During one fight with my wife, she looked at me with tears in her eyes and said something that forever changed the trajectory of my life, my marriage, and my family legacy: "Jerrad, I want you to know that I've been waking up at two every morning. I set my alarm to wake me up in the middle of the night, I go into the living room, and I beg God to capture your heart again."

I was ready to fight that day; she was ready to seek redemption. That was the day God started to break down the walls in my heart and draw me back to him.

Honestly, Leila had every right to leave me. In fact, during that season of our marriage, she even had friends encouraging her to leave me. "There are plenty of fish in the sea, Leila. You're too young and life is too short for you to be unhappy," they'd say.

And in some ways, they were right. But I will never forget how Leila responded: "I'm not leaving Jerrad, because God did not leave me in my mess."

Her response toward me, both in her actions and her words, gave me the clearest glimpse of the gospel I had ever seen. In that moment, I was fully known and fully loved at the same time. Leila saw me at my worst and said, "I'm not going anywhere."

> In that moment, I was fully known and fully loved at the same time.

And this, my friends, is what marriage is all about: two broken people who constantly point each other back to the good news of Jesus by saying, "I know you fully, and I choose to love you fully."

This is spiritual intimacy. Two souls fully exposed to one another, giving each other a glimpse of the God who created them.

Friends, your marriage isn't just for your joy. God didn't pair you with your spouse just to make you happy. He didn't pair you together because it makes more sense financially, or because he knew you needed a travel partner. He paired you together so you can be fully known and fully loved at the same time and so your marriage would serve as a constant reminder that you are fully known and fully loved by your Father.

So with this new goal in mind, here are three ways you can grow in spiritual intimacy with your wife:

PRAY TOGETHER OFTEN.

Prayer has a way of exposing our hidden idols and turning our worship back to the One to whom it belongs. When you pray, you'll often find yourself saying things to God that may have otherwise been hard to say directly to your wife. In that way, you are submitting yourself to a Savior who is better than you and unveiling what is in the depths of your heart. The same is true for your wife. I often learn more about Leila and what is going on in her heart by listening and joining her in prayer. When we pray together, we are recognizing that we aren't just husband and wife. Instead, we are united together as a son and daughter of the Most High. We are both God's children in need of Dad's wisdom and guidance.

> **The key ingredient to intimacy is vulnerability.**

STUDY GOD'S WORD TOGETHER.

The key ingredient to intimacy is vulnerability. I would argue that you can't be truly intimate in any area unless you are willing to first be vulnerable. And here's the truth: There are very few things more vulnerable than having your shortcomings exposed, which is exactly what the Word of God does. It first reveals our brokenness, and then it offers us hope in the middle of our mess. Check out this verse from Hebrews:

> The word of God is living and active, sharper than any two-edged sword, piercing to the division of soul and of spirit, of joints and of marrow, and discerning the thoughts and intentions of the heart (Hebrews 4:12).

Want to be vulnerable with your wife? Study the Word of God together and allow it to expose your thoughts and the intentions of your heart.

Want to be vulnerable with your wife?
Study the Word of God together and
allow it to expose your thoughts
and the intentions of your heart.

Yikes. Showing that kind of vulnerability takes a real man with some serious guts.

Or what about this one from 2 Timothy:

> All Scripture is breathed out by God and profitable for teaching, for reproof, for correction, and for training in righteousness, that the man of God may be complete, equipped for every good work (2 Timothy 3:16-17).

It's one thing to be corrected by your wife or your boss. But you go to another level when you are corrected by God himself.

And yet here is where spiritual intimacy begins to form: when a husband humbly admits in front of his wife that he is not always right and gladly allows the Word of God to expose his sin and shortcomings, knowing that as a result, he will become the man his wife, family, and community need him to be.

Confess to each other.

Most guys would skip this section. For many, it will be too hard to hear.

Brother, don't take the wide path that most guys will take (Matthew 7:13). Take the narrow path, the path that leads to life. The path with a lake at the end of it, filled with deeper intimacy with your wife and God. This path is harder to take, but it is the only one that will truly satisfy your soul.

It is impossible for you to be fully loved unless you are fully known.

Your wife may try to love you fully but not know you fully. In this situation, you aren't receiving the full extent of love that God wants you to receive. Remember, his goal for your marriage is for your wife to give you a glimpse of his love for you. For this to happen, you must be fully known and fully loved.

Practice regular confession to one another, slowly peeling back the veil

> It is impossible for you to be fully loved unless you are fully known.

of your soul. Confess the daily sins. The lie you told at work, the woman you quickly lusted after in the grocery store. Every time you confess your sins, you give your spouse an opportunity to see you fully and love you fully. This kind of "fully seen and fully loved" practice will point you back to the gospel and lead to a level of intimacy that most couples will never experience.

Physical Intimacy: Loving Your Wife with Your Strength

Did you skip the previous sections and come straight to the physical intimacy part?

"Just tell me how to have more sex in my marriage, Jerrad!" I can almost hear you shouting at the book.

If we're honest, it's a little bit of a metaphor for how many of us treat the topic of intimacy within our marriages. We want to get straight to the physical part without first making sure that we are connected on every other level with our spouses.

Sex is one of the greatest gifts that God gave us humans, but it's way more than just a physical act. It's deeper than the connecting of two human bodies. Rather, it's the joining of two souls. It's the culmination of two souls that have first connected emotionally, spiritually, and intellectually.

When I first met Leila, I would ask her a million questions as I tried to get to know her better.

"What's your favorite food?" I once asked.

"Um, either Persian or some kind of pasta," she responded.

"Nice! Mine is Mexican. I could eat Mexican food every day!" I told her.

"I'm not really a big fan of Mexican food," she said with a serious look on her face.

I sat in silence.

I mean, I really liked this girl, but how in the world could I possibly marry someone who doesn't like Mexican food? "Um. Wow. Okay." I frantically searched for some appropriate words to respond. "Maybe you just haven't eaten at the right places," I finally said.

I grew up in California. Leila grew up in Oregon. I soon learned that it's much easier to find authentic Mexican food in California than it is in Oregon.

Soon after getting married, I was determined to show Leila some quality authentic Mexican food, so I took her to my old stomping grounds back in California. We pulled up to a small taco truck in the middle of a random parking lot and ordered a dozen street tacos, with a variety of meats.

"Whoa," she said after her first bite.

"You like it?" I asked.

"That is seriously amazing. I've never had Mexican food like this," she said as she wiped some cilantro off her cheek.

"You see! There's a difference!"

After twelve years of marriage, Leila has now added quality Mexican food to her list of favorites.

So why am I talking about Mexican food in a chapter about physical intimacy? I'll cut straight to the point: You may be experiencing sex in your marriage without experiencing true intimacy. There's a difference.

Whether you're having sex with your spouse daily, once a month, or even a few times a year, if two souls aren't deeply connected, you're missing out on what God has for you.

Leila thought she had tasted real Mexican food, but she hadn't really.

Perhaps you thought you were intimate with your spouse, but you haven't experienced true intimacy. Maybe you've been so focused on just having more sex, you've missed out on a much deeper connection with your spouse.

Sometimes I have to put on my "Linda" voice (from the pet store) and remind myself, "You know you're going to kill your marriage, right?"

"What do you mean?"

"Well, if you think sex is all you need to have a healthy marriage, you're setting yourself up to fail."

Intimacy is more like a betta fish tank than a goldfish tank. Oversimplify it, and you may find the goldfish (the intimacy in marriage) has died. But put in the hard work it requires, and you'll stand back and look at something beautiful.

> **Don't settle for less than what God has planned for your marriage.**

The deep and true intimacy that God has planned for you and your wife is better than a goldfish. It's better than crummy Mexican food. He wants you to experience and enjoy the real stuff.

Great intimacy isn't just great sex. It's great sex as a result of two souls who have deeply connected. This is God's best for you.

If you want to be the spiritual leader of your home, think beyond physical intimacy. Be willing to put in the hard work to connect with your spouse in every other way.

Don't settle for less than what God has planned for your marriage. Put in the hard work of pursuing your spouse the way that God has pursued you, and you'll most likely start to step into new areas of intimacy that you didn't think were possible. Married Christian couples should be having the best sex in the world because we have the gift of being deeply connected at the deepest levels of our souls.

I pray this is the kind of intimacy you enjoy in your marriage.

QUESTIONS TO CONSIDER

1. When you think of the four components of intimacy, which area do you and your wife struggle with the most: emotional, intellectual, spiritual, or physical?

2. What about you personally? In what area is it hardest for you and your wife to connect? Why do you think that is?

3. Go through the four different components. What would it look like for you to grow in each of these areas with your wife?

HOW CAN I STAY CLOSE TO MY WIFE WHEN WE'VE JUST HAD A BABY?

Leila and I have been married for just over twelve years at the time of this writing. She has been pregnant for three of those nearly twelve years. I don't mean she's had three pregnancies (we have four kids). I mean, quite literally, she has been pregnant for thirty-six months of our marriage. Four pregnancies, nine months each.

In addition to the thirty-six months of her carrying babies, we have had infants in our home for four years. And she has nursed babies a total of thirty-six to forty-four months.

In case you're losing track of the math, she has been pregnant, nursing, and/or raising an infant for seven of our twelve years of marriage. Nearly two-thirds of our marriage, so far, has been spent carrying, feeding, and raising babies.

She would be the first to tell you that these didn't feel like the "sexiest" years of our marriage. In fact, as I'm writing these words, she is nursing our eight-month-old and trying to wrangle our two-year-old for lunch.

I'll be honest—the first two pregnancies and subsequent infant years were really hard for me as a husband. I went from being a newlywed groom, getting all the attention of my bride, to feeling like I got put on the back burner while my wife focused on our babies. I knew that she was doing what any mother would and should do, but it didn't stop me from feeling a sense of loneliness, rejection, and at times, even resentment.

I imagine that if you're a father reading this right now, you can likely relate to those same feelings. In fact, I talk to many young dads who are starting to feel a sense of bitterness toward their wives.

"I wish I got as much attention from my wife as our babies do," I've heard on more than one occasion. Maybe you've even had similar thoughts yourself.

I remember one season of life where I was feeling especially frustrated in my marriage. It wasn't necessarily aimed directly toward my wife but more toward our general current circumstances. We had just had our second baby and were trying to navigate the new reality of raising an active two-year-old boy while simultaneously caring for an infant. We hadn't been on a date in months, we hadn't slept through the night in what felt like an eternity, our house was a disaster, we had no rhythm as a family, and we most certainly were not connecting romantically.

We were both mom tired and dad tired, and the truth is, I was starting to get grumpy.

During one chaotic weekend, I can recall frantically trying to get out of the house on time to make it to church. My son was running around naked while I was changing my newborn daughter's outfit for the third time due to diaper blowouts and spit-up catastrophes. Leila was trying to finish putting on her makeup as quickly as possible and complaining that she had nothing to wear.

Does this scene sound familiar?

By the time we got to church, checked the kids into the nursery, and sat down to hear the message, I was exhausted. I mean seriously exhausted. To the point where I couldn't keep my eyes open as the pastor spoke.

I wasn't paying the least bit of attention; I was just happy to have a short break from being a tired dad.

As I sat there trying to keep my eyes open, I felt like the pastor started yelling at me. He didn't really yell, but for whatever reason, the verse he read broke through the white noise that was numbing my brain at the moment. It was almost as if he unintentionally slapped me back into consciousness.

> Husbands, love your wives, as Christ loved the church and gave himself up for her, that he might sanctify her, having cleansed her by the washing of water with the word, so that he might present the church to himself in splendor, without spot or wrinkle or any such thing, that she might be holy and without blemish. In the same way husbands should love their wives as their own bodies. He who loves his wife loves himself. For no one ever hated his own flesh, but nourishes and cherishes it, just as Christ does the church, because we are members of his body. "Therefore a man shall leave his father and mother and hold fast to his wife, and the two shall become one flesh." This mystery is profound, and I am saying that it refers to Christ and the church. However, let each one of you love his wife as himself, and let the wife see that she respects her husband (Ephesians 5:25-33).

I had heard this verse a million times before and had even preached messages from it. But for whatever reason, the Holy Spirit used that verse in that moment to pierce into my soul.

Thank goodness God doesn't love you the way you've been loving your wife. That thought immediately popped into my head out of nowhere, and I was convicted to my core.

At the foundation of my bitterness and frustration was this thought: *I'm*

Jesus loved his bride by essentially saying, *How can I give myself up for her?*

not getting what I want. And this, my friends, is the exact opposite of how Christ looked at us.

When God looked at the brokenness of humanity, he didn't say to himself, *Look at them; they aren't giving me what I want.* Instead, he humbled himself, gave up the luxuries of heaven, and came to serve us in our brokenness.

In short, Jesus loved his bride by essentially saying, *How can I give myself up for her?*

This was the start of God graciously discipling my heart and making it more like his. He was taking my selfishness, rooted in sin, and forming me into his image and likeness.

> Therefore, if anyone is in Christ, he is a new creation. The old has passed away; behold, the new has come (2 Corinthians 5:17).

I left church that day with a tired body but a refreshed soul. I recognized that to be the spiritual leader God is calling me to be, I must first set aside my own preferences for the sake of my bride. I must love her as much as I love myself, knowing God has made us one flesh.

Brother, there will be many seasons of life where we are called to die to ourselves. This is the call of every Christian. Christ gave himself up for his bride and then asked us to do the same.

If your wife has recently had a baby and you feel disconnected from her, I would like to leave you with these two challenges.

First, your marriage is not about you; it is about God. He is using your marriage for your good and for his glory. He will use everything, but especially the hard stuff, to shape you to become more like him. As you feel pieces of you "dying," use them as a reminder to push closer to Jesus and remember that he gave himself up for

> **Your marriage is not about you; it is about God.**

you. Pray, *God, during this season, will you teach me to love my bride with the same selflessness in which you loved me?*

Second, physical romance may be lacking during this season, but that doesn't mean all intimacy should be lost. Remember, physical intimacy is just one component of intimacy in a marriage. Pursue your bride emotionally, intellectually, and spiritually. Most likely, she will need you to lead in these areas more than ever before. We know that there are so many hormones present during the months after a baby is born (in both women and men, by the way). Now is the time to pursue her heart even more deeply. Ask her how she is doing (do this often). Pray for her and your new baby regularly. Engage in the topics she is most curious about during this time.

> Do not make long-term conclusions in the middle of a short-term season.

Last, and maybe most importantly, do not make long-term conclusions in the middle of a short-term season. These newborn and baby phases will come and go. They will be over before you know it. I've seen too many men jump to dramatic conclusions about their wife, their marriage, and even their children in the middle of a hard season. Don't do it, brother. Serve your wife and family the way Jesus served you. Ask God to give you his servant's heart during this time in your family. Pursue intimacy on deeper levels. And whatever you do, don't make long-term conclusions in a short-term season.

BREAKFAST TABLE PRAYERS

How Should I Pray with My Kids?

If you're a dad, you probably remember the day you brought home your first child.

Wasn't that a crazy feeling?

I remember the hospital staff handing me my son and telling us we were free to go home.

"Don't I need to pass a new parent test, or something?" I asked the nurse.

She laughed.

"No, I'm serious. Are you really going to send us home with this baby already? Do you have a brochure or something?"

When Leila and I arrived home, the chaos of our new reality immediately sank in. Most of those early days are a blur to me, but I do remember not leaving the house for the first couple of weeks. On any given day, I wouldn't have been able to tell you what day of the week it was, what time it was, or even the last time I ate or showered. Everything blended together—we were merely trying to survive.

I'll never forget one night after we had been rotating feeding and diaper-changing shifts all day while the other person tried to sneak in a few quick minutes of rest. We were absolutely exhausted. Leila had just finished nursing Elijah and putting him to bed for the night. I remember praying quietly in my head, asking God to give us at least two or three solid hours of sleep. My silent prayers quickly led to me dosing off and falling into a much-needed sleep.

I couldn't have been asleep more than ten minutes when I woke up to the sound of crying. I quickly sat up, thinking it was my newborn son until I realized the sobs were actually coming from the other side of the bed.

"Babe, are you okay?" I asked Leila, putting my hand on her shoulder.

My simple question to her opened up the floodgates. She began fully sobbing.

At this point, I started to become genuinely concerned. *Did I miss a death in the family or something?* I wondered. I had no idea what was going on.

"Hey, babe, what's going on?" I started to rub her back.

She turned her face into her pillow as the tears continued to flow.

For several minutes, I waited anxiously for her to compose herself. Finally, after what felt like an eternity, she was able to get these words out:

"I just…I just…I don't know. I just feel like we're failing our son," she said through the sobs.

My heart sank. Was I failing as a dad already?

"What do you mean?" I asked her.

"I mean, have we even prayed with him? Does he even know Jesus? Are we even raising him to be a godly young man?"

I'll be honest, at this point, I was just confused. *Whoa. Postpregnancy hormones are crazy,* I thought. Truthfully, I wanted to laugh, but the timing didn't feel right for that either.

"Hey, babe, I just want to make sure we're on the same page. We're talking about our two-and-a-half-week-old son, right?" I asked in the most noncondescending way possible.

"Yes!" she quickly responded. "We need to be praying with him more!" She was raising her voice a little.

I highly recommend not doing what I did next, but I couldn't help myself at this point: I immediately burst into laughter.

"Babe, I love you so much, but I think we're doing okay so far. He's just a couple weeks old. We haven't slept in days, if not weeks. We'll get this whole thing figured out, but for right now, we should rest." I continued to rub her back.

She took a deep breath, closed her eyes, and almost immediately fell asleep.

Well, that was weird, I thought before joining her for some much-needed rest.

Since you're reading this chapter, you most likely feel like you have room to grow when it comes to praying more with your kids. Maybe not to the point of crying yourself to sleep about it, but I'm sure it's crossed your mind a time or two.

If that's true, just know you're not alone.

I recently asked the guys in our Dad Tired community to honestly assess how they're doing when it comes to praying with their kids and how often they do it. Here are some of their answers:

- "We don't. Part of it is I've never felt comfortable about praying. Another part is this was never modeled for me growing up."

- "Definitely not enough....Probably because I don't pray consistently myself."

- "Not very often, as I work late, and they are in bed before I get home. The problem is, prayer has not been a very big part of my life. I think my wife does more than me, so it is a letdown in that way."

- "Not like I should. Seems like I did more when they were younger. Why? Not sure, other than just not being intentional."

Can you relate to any of that? I know I can.

For some guys, the thought of praying with their kids feels totally foreign because they were never taught how to do it as children. They never had a dad who sat and prayed with them, and now they feel completely uncomfortable at the thought of trying to pray with their own kids. It simply feels forced or awkward. Or maybe both.

> It's hard to model something that you have little experience in. There are very few things guys hate more than feeling incompetent.

Maybe you can relate to the comment about not praying enough by yourself. Trust me, it's hard to model something that you have little experience in. There are very few things guys hate more than feeling incompetent. And for many of us, we don't know how to pray out loud with our kids because we spend very little time praying alone by ourselves.

You may feel like it's something you don't necessarily need to be intentional about because your wife seems to have it covered. *She's better at praying than I am*, you think to yourself, so you just let her take the lead.

No matter where you land on that spectrum, the reality is this: Your family desperately needs a father who will lead them to the better Father by praying out loud with them and doing it often.

Your family desperately needs a father who will lead them to the better Father by praying out loud with them and doing it often.

Q&A MIXTAPE

As dads, we know that our primary role is to raise disciples who love and act like Jesus by the time they grow into adulthood. Ultimately, we must trust their spiritual journey to the Lord, but to the best of our ability, we want to train them to learn and walk in the ways of Jesus. So whenever I feel stuck on a certain parenting or discipleship issue, I try to always go back to the ultimate disciple-maker: Jesus himself. If we want our children to be like Jesus, we must know who Jesus really is.

> **If we want our children to be like Jesus, we must know who Jesus really is.**

I recently read through the Gospels again, specifically looking for all the ways Jesus prayed. I've read plenty of books on the topic of prayer. I've listened to countless messages on prayer. But I wanted to hear from the King himself. How did he pray?

The first time I encountered Jesus praying was in Matthew 14, right before the famous story where he feeds a crowd of 5,000 men (plus women and children) with five loaves of bread and two fish. His disciples were trying to convince him to let the crowd go so they could find something to eat. But Jesus had other plans:

> But Jesus said, "They need not go away; you give them something to eat." They said to him, "We have only five loaves here and two fish." And he said, "Bring them here to me." Then he ordered the crowds to sit down on the grass, and taking the five loaves and the two fish, *he looked up to heaven and said a blessing.* Then he broke the loaves and gave them to the disciples, and the disciples gave them to the crowds. And they all ate and were satisfied. And they took up twelve baskets full of the broken pieces left over. And those who ate

were about five thousand men, besides women and children (Matthew 14:16-21).

The second time we see Jesus pray is almost immediately after he feeds the crowd, right before his next miracle of walking on water. Take a look:

> Immediately he made the disciples get into the boat and go before him to the other side, while he dismissed the crowds. And after he had dismissed the crowds, *he went up on the mountain by himself to pray.* When evening came, he was there alone, but the boat by this time was a long way from the land, beaten by the waves, for the wind was against them. And in the fourth watch of the night he came to them, walking on the sea. But when the disciples saw him walking on the sea, they were terrified, and said, "It is a ghost!" and they cried out in fear. But immediately Jesus spoke to them, saying, "Take heart; it is I. Do not be afraid" (Matthew 14:22-27).

Okay, so if you were reading the Gospels in the order they are arranged in your Bible, you would see in Matthew 14 that Jesus seems to pray right before and right after performing some of his miracles. In fact, all throughout the Gospels, we read about how often Jesus prayed. We learn that sometimes he prayed in front of his disciples, giving thanks for the food, while other times he broke away from the crowds to spend some time alone in prayer. At this point, we're learning a little bit about Jesus's prayer life, but there's just one big problem in our research: Even though we know that Jesus is praying, we don't know *what* he is praying.

I wanted to his hear words. What was he saying as he talked with his Father?

To answer that question, I had to dig deeper. And as it turns out, there are only a few short records of Jesus's actual prayers. Here are a few:

- "When Jesus had spoken these words, he lifted up his eyes to heaven, and said, 'Father, the hour has come; glorify your Son that the Son may glorify you, since you have given him authority over all flesh, to give eternal life to all whom you have given him. And this is eternal life, that they know you, the only true God, and Jesus Christ whom you have sent. I glorified you on earth, having accomplished the work that you gave me to do. And now, Father, glorify me in your own presence with the glory that I had with you before the world existed'" (John 17:1-5).

- "Father, glorify your name" (John 12:28).

- "Jesus lifted up his eyes and said, 'Father, I thank you that you have heard me. I knew that you always hear me, but I said this on account of the people standing around, that they may believe that you sent me'" (John 11:41-42).

- "Going a little farther he fell on his face and prayed, saying, 'My Father, if it be possible, let this cup pass from me; nevertheless, not as I will, but as you will'" (Matthew 26:39).

And finally, he said these prayers while he was dying on a cross:

- "Jesus said, 'Father, forgive them, for they know not what they do'" (Luke 23:34).

- "About the ninth hour Jesus cried out with a loud voice, saying, 'Eli, Eli, lema sabachthani?' that is, 'My God, my God, why have you forsaken me?'" (Matthew 27:46).

- "Then Jesus, calling out with a loud voice, said, 'Father, into your hands I commit my spirit!' And having said this he breathed his last" (Luke 23:46).

Okay, I can already hear you saying, "Jerrad, where are we going with all this?"

I know we jumped all over the place, and I know that was a lot of Scripture to read at once. But I want you to catch something important. After reading through the Gospels, here are some conclusions I've made about the way Jesus prayed: His prayers were short, his prayers were spontaneous, and his prayers were authentic.

> **The way Jesus prayed was often the opposite of how we pray.**

I point this out because if you're like me or like most of the men in our Dad Tired community, it's hard not to notice that the way Jesus prayed was often the opposite of how we pray, or how we believe we are supposed to pray.

Let me put it another way. Have you ever found yourself hesitant to pray with your kids because you don't feel like you know exactly what to say? Or maybe you get paralyzed by the thought of not being consistent with a good prayer-time routine? Or maybe you just don't feel like praying because your prayers have become robotic; you feel like they are lacking genuine authenticity, and you say the same prayers time after time.

If you relate to any of that, let me give you some good news.

Spiritual leaders lead and pray like Jesus. How did Jesus pray? Well, first, his prayers were often short. In fact, after reading every recorded prayer of his in the Scriptures, you'd be hard-pressed to find one that lasted more than thirty seconds. I guess he was serious when he told his disciples not to pray long-winded prayers:

> When you pray, do not heap up empty phrases as the Gentiles do, for they think that they will be heard for their many words. Do not be like them, for your Father knows what you need before you ask him (Matthew 6:7-8).

Spiritual leaders lead
and pray like Jesus.

Do you want to be an obedient spiritual leader and pray like Jesus? Stop worrying about how long your prayers are. Instead, pray short and simple prayers with your kids.

Second, when studying the Scriptures, we learn that Jesus's prayers were often spontaneous. Too many of us dads get paralyzed from being intentional with our family because we are afraid we can't stick with new rhythms and habits.

I don't even want to try to implement prayer times with my kids because I know I'll eventually fall off the wagon, you might think. You've been convinced that it's better not to start than to start and fail.

> **Pray short and simple prayers with your kids.**

Here's the good news: Yes, it's true that Jesus broke away to be alone in prayer, but most of his prayers that we see in Scripture were spontaneous. He prayed before he ate, he prayed before miracles, and he prayed to teach his disciples how to pray. There was no magic formula or model to follow. Instead, we often see Jesus spontaneously going before the Father.

Last week we had some friends staying at our house for a few days. During breakfast one morning, one of my friends was sharing with us how she was struggling mentally, repeatedly getting stuck believing the lies of the evil one. She had been convinced that she was invaluable and no longer had a purpose on this earth. With tears filling her eyes, she looked at me and said, "Please just keep me in your prayers. I'm really struggling."

"I will absolutely continue to pray for you, but I'd like to pray with you right now, if that's okay," I said.

I looked over at my son, who was eating a bowl of cereal. I could tell he was sensing the weight of the conversation happening in front of him.

"Come put your hand on her," I said to him. "Let's pray now."

My son, my wife, and I each laid our hands on our friend and began to pray God's truth over her. By the time we were done, we were all emotional as we sensed the peace of God with us at the breakfast table.

Now, let me tell you, I've prayed dozens of prayers with my kids before we've eaten a meal or gone to bed, but I can assure you that this spontaneous prayer, along with the many others we have shared as a family, will stick with them much deeper than those said during our routine prayer times.

Yes, brother, pray with your kids before meals and before they go to bed. But don't forget to be like Jesus when it comes to praying with your family. Pray spontaneously. Pray when they least expect it. Go to the Father when they get hurt, when they're scared, when they're stuck on a problem, and when you sense God's goodness on display right in front of you.

> **Spiritual leaders pray spontaneously as often as possible.**

Spiritual leaders pray spontaneously as often as possible.

Finally, as we study the way Jesus prayed, we see that his prayers were not only short and spontaneous; they were also authentic. Jesus prayed when he was scared (Matthew 26:39). Jesus prayed when his enemies were against him (Luke 23:34). And Jesus prayed when he felt abandoned by the Father (Matthew 27:46).

Don't fall into the trap of thinking that your kids need to only hear you pray neat, clean, and fancy prayers. They don't. In fact, they need to hear a dad who is desperate for God to show up. They need to know that Daddy isn't the hero of the family, Jesus is, and that even Daddy needs help. Obviously, it goes without saying that we are to be sensitive to what our children can handle and at what age they should be exposed to certain things. But I promise you, you will raise disciples who look a lot more like Jesus when they have a daddy who prays authentically with them. Many of the best prayer times I've had with my kids have come when I've said, "Daddy doesn't know what to do right now; pray with me that God would give us his wisdom."

Brother, I don't know what lies you're believing when it comes to praying with your kids, but I urge you to come back to the truth of the Scriptures. Follow the ways of Jesus. Like him, keep your prayers short, spontaneous, and authentic. If it was good enough for him and his disciples, it is more than sufficient for you and your family.

QUESTIONS TO CONSIDER

1. What prevents you from praying more often with your kids?

2. Stop and reflect on your life right now. Where are you desperate for God to show up? Do you need him to provide for your family? Give you the courage to confess a sin? Help with overcoming a habit or addiction? Take those things to the Lord right now.

3. Do you find yourself praying more during specific times (morning, dinner, bedtime) or spontaneously? Do you feel comfortable spontaneously praying with your wife and kids? If not, is it something you'd be willing to try this week?

WHERE'S DINNER?

How Can I Consistently Connect with My Kids?

Last week I was wrapping up a full day of meetings when Leila called.

"Hey Jer,[1] can you grab dinner for the kids on your way home? It's been a long day, and I haven't had a chance to make anything."

"No problem, babe. Should be done here shortly, and then I'll make my way home."

We said our goodbyes, and I went back to finish my meeting.

About forty minutes later, I walked in the door and greeted the family with all kinds of hugs and kisses.

"What'd you get us for dinner, Daddy?" my second daughter yelled as I picked her up in my arms.

"What's that?"

"What did you get us for dinner? We're starving!" she repeated.

I could feel Leila's eyeballs piercing a hole in the side of my head as I stood in silence.

---

1. If any of you try to call me that, I will immediately block you. This name is reserved exclusively for my wife.

"Yeah, babe. What did you get the kids for dinner?" Leila asked, knowing full well what was going on in the moment.

I had completely dropped the ball.

"I am so sorry. I totally forgot to pick something up. I'll go grab something now!"

I could feel the whole family's disappointment filling the room.

"How could you forget? I literally just asked you about it less than an hour ago," Leila said with frustration in her voice.

Here's the truth: Not only did I forget to grab dinner; I barely remembered my short call with her only moments earlier. I couldn't even remember what happened on my drive home. I didn't remember what the traffic was like, I didn't remember the weather, and I obviously didn't remember the instructions I had been given about dinner. Yes, I made it home, but I had no idea what happened in between. I was in complete autopilot mode.

Have you ever felt like you were on autopilot mode as a dad?

I usually feel it at night, right before I fall asleep. *What did I even do today?* I often ask myself.

These are usually the moments where that dad guilt starts to sink in. I'll look back on my day the same way I looked back on the drive home from the meetings: I barely remember any of it. The worst part is, I start to think about how I made it through an entire day without having a single meaningful conversation with any of my kids. An entire day, gone. Wasted. Sure, I may have been productive at work (which only adds salt to the wounds, considering my work is helping dads). But what did I actually accomplish in terms of building my relationship with my kids and connecting with them in deeper ways?

> **Too often as a dad, I find myself in autopilot mode.**

Before I fall asleep, I often ask God
to help me be the kind of dad he
is to me. To help me father their
hearts the way he is fathering mine.

Q&A MIXTAPE

Too often as a dad, I find myself in autopilot mode. I make it through the day but show up to my destination empty-handed.

These nights typically end with me making a commitment to myself to try harder to be a better father the next day. Before I fall asleep, I often ask God to help me be the kind of dad he is to me. To help me father their hearts the way he is fathering mine.

The other day, Jesus answered that prayer.

Well, he at least added some clarity to it for me. Let me explain.

NOT ALWAYS MIRACULOUS, BUT ALWAYS PRESENT

I was in Michigan, getting ready to speak at a men's retreat. I was in my room, putting the finishing touches on a message I had given several times before at various men's events. The title of the message was "Breakfast Is Ready," and it tells the story of Jesus's radical grace put on display for Peter, just days after Peter had denied he even knew Jesus. Instead of bailing on Peter or holding a grudge against him, Jesus cooks him breakfast. In the middle of Peter's worst week, after one of his worst decisions, Jesus is making his friend breakfast. It's one of the most beautiful and tangible displays of grace we see in the Scriptures. It reminds us that even on our worst day, Jesus shows up.

In my first book, *Dad Tired and Loving It: Stumbling Your Way to Spiritual Leadership*, I give a more in-depth argument on why I believe God consistently displays this radical grace throughout Scripture. As amazing as it was to see Jesus making breakfast for his friend, even after he denied him, it wasn't necessarily new. God had been showing up among his people from the very first pages of Scripture.

In case you haven't had a chance to read that first book or maybe need a quick refresher, let's look at some of the key Scriptures that clue us in on who God is and the reputation he has among his children.

The first comes right from the very first pages of the story, in the book of Genesis. God had created everything exactly as he designed it to be; it was all perfect. Humans were interacting with one another exactly the way God intended. Their relationship with him, their Creator, was also perfect; exactly as he designed it to be. There was no friction, or shame, or confusion. They were his children, and he was their father.

It's beautiful, isn't it?

Well, it lasts for only about one page in the Bible before things go sideways. You get to Genesis 3 and find humans starting to rebel against God. They believe the lies of the enemy and search for meaning, purpose, and identity outside of their father.

> Now the serpent was more crafty than any other beast of the field that the Lord God had made.
>
> He said to the woman, "Did God actually say, 'You shall not eat of any tree in the garden'?" And the woman said to the serpent, "We may eat of the fruit of the trees in the garden, but God said, 'You shall not eat of the fruit of the tree that is in the midst of the garden, neither shall you touch it, lest you die.'" But the serpent said to the woman, "You will not surely die. For God knows that when you eat of it your eyes will be opened, and you will be like God, knowing good and evil." So when the woman saw that the tree was good for food, and that it was a delight to the eyes, and that the tree was to be desired to make one wise, she took of its fruit and ate, and she also gave some to her husband who was with her, and he ate. Then the eyes of both were opened, and they knew that they were naked. And they sewed fig leaves together and made themselves loincloths (Genesis 3:1-7).

Now, if you were new to the Bible, you'd probably guess what likely happens next. When our kids are blatantly disobedient, we typically don't handle it so well. Surely God the Father is the same, right?

Well, you might be surprised. Look how he responds:

> And they heard the sound of the Lord God walking in the garden in the cool of the day, and the man and his wife hid themselves from the presence of the Lord God among the trees of the garden. But the Lord God called to the man and said to him, "Where are you?" (Genesis 3:8-9).

This passage always amazes me. The way God fathers his children in this scene looks so different from the way I often parent my kids. I can't tell you the number of times I've yelled at my kids from another room as I listen to them argue or disobey. Honestly, I just kind of subconsciously assume that is how God would parent his children.

But we don't see God shouting from heaven. What does he do instead?

He takes a walk. In the cool of the day. It's almost as if the writer wants to contrast the chaos of Adam and Eve's disobedience with the calmness of the Father.

As the whole world starts to fall apart, from the micro to the macro, God is walking among his children in the cool of the day. God isn't shouting from heaven. God is *with* them.

> **It's starting to seem like God really enjoys being with his children.**

This shouldn't surprise us because God always wants to be near his people.

Fast-forward in your Bible to Exodus 25. Here we have a large group of God's children who are constantly trying to decide if they want to follow and obey him or if they want to put their hope in golden statues.

Imagine your kids being so rebellious that they deny you as their father and instead put their trust in a golden cow. You'd likely freak out, right? That's not what God the Father does. Look at verse 8:

Let them make me a sanctuary, that I may dwell in their midst (Exodus 25:8).

It's starting to seem like God really enjoys being with his children.

What about the famous passage in Matthew 1, where the angel tells Joseph that his soon-to-be wife is going to give birth to the Savior of the world (despite being a virgin)? We sing about it every Christmas, so you may be numb to it, but really try to let this reality sink in.

> "She will bear a son, and you shall call his name Jesus, for he will save his people from their sins." All this took place to fulfill what the Lord had spoken by the prophet:
>
> "Behold, the virgin shall conceive and bear a son, and they shall call his name Immanuel" (which means, God with us) (Matthew 1:21-23).

God *with* us.

It doesn't stop there either.

As Jesus began to prepare to die on a cross, his disciples got worried that they were not ready to be left alone. The Jewish people had waited hundreds of years for their messiah to show up, and the thought of him leaving them was too much for them to carry. Listen to Jesus's comforting words:

> If you love me, you will keep my commandments. And I will ask the Father, and he will give you another Helper, to be *with* you forever, even the Spirit of truth, whom the world cannot receive, because it neither sees him nor knows him. You know him, for he dwells *with* you and will be in you.
>
> I will not leave you as orphans; I will come to you. Yet a little while and the world will see me no more, but you will see me. Because I live, you also will live. In that day you will know that I am in my Father, and you in me, and I in you (John 14:15-20).

God with his children in the Garden of Eden and as they wander through the desert. Jesus with his people in flesh and blood. The Holy Spirit with his people after Jesus ascends to heaven.

God is always with his children.

His reputation of being with his children lasts from the very first pages until the very last pages of your Bible. Take a look at one of my favorite passages of all time. It's this verse that brings hope and peace to my soul as a husband, father, and disciple.

> Then I saw a new heaven and a new earth, for the first heaven and the first earth had passed away, and the sea was no more. And I saw the holy city, new Jerusalem, coming down out of heaven from God, prepared as a bride adorned for her husband. And I heard a loud voice from the throne saying, "Behold, the dwelling place of God is *with* man. He will dwell *with* them, and they will be his people, and God himself will be *with* them as their God. He will wipe away every tear from their eyes, and death shall be no more, neither shall there be mourning, nor crying, nor pain anymore, for the former things have passed away" (Revelation 21:1-4).

I know we're supposed to be talking about dad stuff right now, but can we pause for just a minute and talk about gospel stuff?

Brother, don't miss this amazing truth for you personally as a man.

God could have (and maybe should have) bailed on his people at any point, but he didn't.

Let me make it more pointed: God could have (and maybe should have) bailed on *you* at any point. Let's be honest, he's had every right to leave us. But he didn't.

He has a reputation of being *with* his people, and he has a reputation of being with you.

That's good news.

And it's that good news that changes the way we parent our children. We aren't just trying to be more present with our kids because it's the right thing to do. We're trying to be more present with our kids because we want to show them what God is like. Yes, God is amazing for so many reasons. He provides for us, takes care of us, shows off his glory, and even performs unexpected miracles. But you know what's truly amazing? That God is with us. The God of the universe. The all-knowing, all-powerful, all-majestic Creator of all things is *with* us. When you talk to him, he listens. When you need his attention, he is fully present.

This is the reputation of our God. And it's the reputation we all long to have in our families.

You don't need to do anything fancy or miraculous to be a good dad and connect with your children. You simply need to be with them. Fully present with them. Just like your heavenly Father is with you.

PRESENT BUT NOT PRESENT

I'm writing this book in the middle of the global COVID-19 pandemic. I pray that by the time you read this, the chaos of this pandemic will be long behind us.

It's been two years since this all started, but I have vivid memories of when we first heard the news. It was eerie. The streets were empty, and shelves at grocery stores had been cleared out, and no one was allowed to leave their house, in fear that they might catch or spread the virus.

People were trying to make the best of a difficult and scary season. During those early days of the quarantine, I saw this phrase repeated continuously on social media: "I'm going to take advantage of this situation to spend more time with my family."

You don't need to do anything fancy or miraculous to be a good dad and connect with your children. You simply need to be with them. Fully present with them. Just like your heavenly Father is with you.

Q&A MIXTAPE

For the first time in years, and maybe ever, families were finding themselves together more than they had ever been before. Instead of Dad heading off to work, he was now required to work from home.

It was awesome…for about two weeks.

I remember the guys in our Dad Tired community sharing how they were really struggling at home. They admitted that even though they were physically present with their kids, they weren't fully there.

What they were describing hit me square between the eyes the other day while my son and I were sitting on the couch. I was flipping through the channels on the television and paused when I saw the words "News Alert" pop up in bright red letters on the screen.

"Hey Dad, look at this." Elijah was trying to get my attention.

"Hold on, son, let me watch this news alert real quick."

A couple minutes passed. "Dad, check this out."

"Give me a sec, son," I said, growing a little impatient.

More time passed. "Dad, look at this."

"Hold on, son, this is super important information about our world's future."

As those words came out of my mouth, I was immediately convicted in my spirit. I felt like I heard God say, "You're worried about the future of the world when the future of the world is sitting right next to you."

Ouch.

> **I felt like I heard God say, "You're worried about the future of the world when the future of the world is sitting right next to you."**

We have a funny way of getting sucked into "important" things while missing the important things right in front of us.

Can you relate?

As I've traveled the country speaking to men, I often share my story of how my dad left our family when I was three. One of the most common responses I get is this: "My dad never left, but he wasn't fully there. Yeah, he worked hard and provided for our family, but he wasn't really there for me in the ways I needed him most."

I used to think a man leaving a family was the worst thing he could do to them. But honestly, I'm starting to wonder if it's equally as harmful to have a dad who was present but not really present. What would it be like to have a father so close and yet feel like he's a million miles away?

That thought crushes me.

> **The more we interact with the ever-present Father, the more present we earthly fathers become to our kids.**

It crushes me because I know there are times when my children may say the same about me. They know I'm here, but am I actually *with* them?

This is why we must stay connected to the gospel, friends. It is our primary motivation for staying connected to our children. The more we interact with the ever-present Father, the more present we earthly fathers become to our kids.

May we not have the reputation of being dads who are present with our kids but not actually with them. Instead, by God's grace and the power of his gospel, may we have his reputation—that we are always with our children.

THREE PRACTICAL WAYS TO BE PRESENT AND CONNECT WITH YOUR KIDS

I want to share three practical ways that I try to connect with my kids regularly. I pray they are helpful for you on your journey. I'd also love for you to share ways that you've been able to connect with your family. As a reminder, we have a community of men talking about this stuff daily, and we'd love for you to join us.[2]

Birthday Dates

Having four children, it can sometimes feel like I'm coaching a basketball team. I'll be honest: I find myself managing the group as a whole and will often forget to connect with each child one-on-one. One thing that's been super helpful in this regard is scheduling a daddy date with each child on the day they were born each month. My son was born on May 22, so I've blocked off the twenty-second of each month to spend some one-on-one time with him. The same goes for my three girls. Keep in mind, this doesn't need to be big and miraculous for us to father our kids the way God fathers us. It just needs to be intentional. Many times, these dates are as simple as grabbing a donut down the street, taking a walk on a nearby trail, eating at our favorite restaurant, or checking out a local high school sporting event.

Uninterrupted Dinners

This is a drum I will continue to beat over and over until the day I die. I am fully convinced that one of the greatest gifts you can give your family is to be fully present at as many meals as possible. We have a rule in our house that all meals must be eaten together at the table, and none of them can include technology. In fact, most of our dinners are eaten around a candle placed at the center of the table. Many of your best conversations and discipleship moments will be shared over a meal. Don't miss the opportunity to connect with your kids in very simple but profound ways each day. Be *with* them.

Get into What They're Into

Sometimes I have a hard time praying because I convince myself that

---

2. "Home," Dad Tired, connect.dadtired.com.

God has better things to worry about. *Does he even actually care about this?* I often wonder.

The crazy part is, he does. The apostle Paul writes,

> Do not be anxious about anything, but in everything by prayer and supplication with thanksgiving let your requests be made known to God (Philippians 4:6).

God wants to hear your requests. He's the kind of father that wants to know what's on your heart.

One of the best ways to connect with your kids is to give them your full attention on things that matter the most to them. In this way, you show them what the Father is like. My two-year-old will spend fifteen minutes telling me about a *Peppa Pig* episode she just watched. And as much as I want to move past it and get to the million other things I have on my to-do list for that day, I try to discipline myself enough to listen. To give her my full attention in the same way that God gives me his. Because here's the truth: Today she wants to talk about *Peppa Pig*, but soon she will want to talk about a boy she is interested in, a fear that's keeping her up at night, the doubt she is wrestling through in her faith, or the shortcomings she feels as a wife and mom. Being fully with her today assures her that I will be with her for life.

> God has a reputation of being trustworthy in his care for us.

We trust God because he has a reputation of being trustworthy in his care for us. May the same be true of us as fathers.

QUESTIONS TO CONSIDER

1. Think about your own childhood for a minute. Was your father fully present? If not, in what ways do you feel like he wasn't present for you?

2. Reflect on the past seven days with your family. How many moments did you have of meaningful conversation or connection with your kids? Were there any moments you intentionally set up to connect with them?

3. Over the next seven days, what changes can you make to be more fully present with your children? Is there something in your life that you need to give up that is stealing your attention from them?

DIRTY DISHES

Teaching Your Kids How to Fight Well

In chapter 1, I shared how Leila and I had just brought our fourth child home from the hospital. If you have a baby at home, you know the mix of emotions that come with this season of life. On the one hand, it's the most fun, exciting, and joy-filled days you can imagine having as a family. But let's be honest—on the other hand, it is absolutely exhausting.

I remember after having our first, Elijah, I felt like I was going to die from sleep deprivation. I called my mom to try to get some wisdom from a woman who had raised three children by herself.

"This is so hard, Mom. How did you do this alone? I haven't slept in weeks."

"I know it's exhausting, son. But don't worry; it gets easier. In two or three months, he'll be sleeping a lot better." She was trying her best to comfort me.

"Two or three months!" I nearly shouted. "Are you kidding me? There's no way I can do this for another two or three months!"

She had intended to encourage me, but I felt deflated.

You know exactly what I'm talking about if you're a parent. You love that baby with every ounce of your being, but you also love sleep, and living without it feels like you're being tortured as a prisoner of war.

All that to say, we have baby number four in our house right now, and even knowing full well what to expect regarding the kind of sleep we will all be getting over the next several months, it doesn't make it any easier.

The other day, Leila fed Emilia and then immediately started to do the dishes.

"Let me get this, babe. You should go rest," I said.

I'll be honest, my wife is stunning, but in this moment, she looked like she had been dragged through a knothole backward. She hadn't had a good rest in quite some time, and I knew the greatest gift I could give her was some quiet time while I took on the chores of the house.

She reluctantly took me up on my offer and went to lay down on the couch.

As she slowly drifted off to sleep, I put on my noise-canceling headphones and listened to some music while finishing up the dirty pile of dishes in the sink. I was about two songs into my worship playlist when the faint sounds of screaming cut their way through the noise-canceling technology.

I slipped one headphone off my ear to get a better sense of what was going on. As I listened more closely, I could hear intense arguing coming from my two older kids as they played with LEGOs in a bedroom upstairs.

"Give me the yellow piece!"

"No! You have enough yellow pieces! You need to start learning how to share for once in your life!"

With every sentence, the two of them got louder and louder.

I'm not going to sugarcoat this story for you. I lost my stuff.

Is there anything more embarrassing than going from being in the presence of God while listening to worship music and doing the dishes to absolutely losing your cool and screaming at your kids within the span of ten seconds?

Not only that, I was trying to scream at them quietly so I wouldn't wake our baby or my wife. If you're not a parent, that might not make sense to you. But all my parent friends know what it's like to scream at your kids at the top of your lungs in a "whisper" type voice. It's an art, really.

"You two need to quit it right now!" I shouted at the top of my whisper-voice. "Your mom and sister are sleeping, and if you wake them up over LEGOs, I'm going to absolutely lose it."

The truth is, I think I had already lost it. But I wanted them to think I had a few more layers of anger I could pour out to them.

And it worked. They immediately got quiet.

I slipped the headphones back over my ear, grabbed another dirty dish, and went back to worshipping the Prince of Peace.[1]

I kid you not, I didn't even make it through the next song when a "ding" interrupted the music, alerting me that I had a new text message.

I wiped my hands dry with a towel, pulled out the phone from my pocket, and read this message: "Hey, man. Do you have a minute to text? I'm struggling." It was from one of the students in our Family Leadership Program.[2]

I shot back a reply. "Of course, dude. What's going on?"

> **God is always trying to discipline our hearts as men.**

"My wife and I just got into a huge argument. Both of us lost our cool and said some nasty things to each other. I said some things I really regret saying in my anger. I gotta figure out how to do this better, bro. I'm embarrassed by the way I fight sometimes."

I don't like to overspiritualize things, but I have to be honest: Sometimes the timing of things really freaks me out. I'm convinced that God is always

---

1. Yes, I recognize the irony.

2. "Family Leadership Program," Dad Tired, dadtired.com/lead.

trying to discipline our hearts as men, and he will use any and every opportunity to do that.

How weird is it that I had just got done screaming at my kids for arguing, and then minutes later, a guy reaches out to me asking for help because of the way he and his wife argue?

God was using this moment to parent my heart. That's what he always does; he parents our hearts. He's a good father.

Before I could even respond to the text, this thought immediately came into my mind. I'm convinced it was inspired by the Holy Spirit: *Jerrad, the goal isn't to teach your kids how to not fight. The goal is to teach them how to fight well.*

I realized in that moment that if I'm not careful, I will raise a son and daughters who never learn how to fight in a God-honoring way. If my parenting strategy is to simply yell at them from the other side of the house and tell them to just "stop it," I have fallen short of parenting their hearts. My role as a disciple-maker is not to just get my kids to behave well; my role is to raise disciples who represent King Jesus. Simply yelling at them and telling them to stop is not discipleship; it's behavior management. And by only managing their behavior, instead of giving them gospel tools, I am setting them up to be in marriages where they, too, will one day not know how to fight with their future spouses.

> **My role as a disciple-maker is not to just get my kids to behave well; my role is to raise disciples who represent King Jesus.**

I won't always be around to just tell them, "Knock it off!" I need to train them to know how to handle conflict well, and in a way that honors the God they serve.

This is spiritual leadership.

I knew at that moment that I had fallen short of leading in that way.

A BOY IN A MAN'S BODY

I'm not going to lie to you: I used to be an absolutely terrible fighter. When I look back on the early days of my marriage, I'm embarrassed at the way I used to handle conflicts with Leila. I fought like an emotionally unstable thirteen-year-old boy trapped in a man's body. If I felt threatened in any way, I would become like a lion backed into a corner—slamming doors and saying hurtful things, just to win an argument. I was completely unreasonable and let my emotions dictate how I handled the situation. In short, I was out of control.

Now, I know we're talking about how to raise children who fight well, but it would be foolish of us to try to teach our kids something that we aren't personally trying to grow in ourselves.

Stop and ask yourself an honest question: Are you a good fighter? When conflict arises, do you fight well?

In my experience of working with men, there are typically two ways a guy tends to lean when getting into some type of disagreement with his wife: Either he fights or he "flights." I'm not necessarily talking about your natural, God-given personality, when you're in the middle of a disagreement with your bride. I'm talking about you at your worst. When you move to an unhealthy place mentally, what road do you go down?

> **Stop and ask yourself an honest question: Are you a good fighter?**

Fighters typically get loud. They convince themselves that their power is in their strength. If they can be loud, aggressive, and verbally intimidating, then they will force their opponent to eventually back down.

"Flighters," on the other hand, use the opposite technique. Their weapon of choice is not volume or hurtful words. Instead, they employ their silence as their ultimate tool.

Now, I've had lots of guys push back on this one and say, "I don't know, Jerrad. I'm naturally a quiet guy, and sometimes my wife can be very aggressive. It's easier for me to just sit back quietly as she gets all her anger out of her system."

Remember, I'm not talking about your natural bent, your God-given personality. I'm talking about you in your unhealthy state of mind.

Being quiet as a way to gather your thoughts, listen carefully, and make a wise choice is not sinful or wrong. But being silent as a way to manipulate your partner most certainly is.

Honestly, in my unhealthy ways, I've used both weapons against my wife. Both are equally painful, sinful, and destructive to our marriage.

There have been times where I've shown up ready to fight and have said deeply hurtful words to my bride. I carry the weight of guilt to this day for some of the things I've said to her.

At other times, I've purposely remained silent as a way to keep her guessing what I was thinking. This tactic only puts a wall between you and your spouse. Even though you're not saying hurtful words that you'll later wish you could take back, you are still causing a great deal of pain and friction.

Let me be super clear: Being quiet is not wrong. It is okay to say to your wife, "I hear what you're saying, but I want to take some time to better understand. Would it be okay if I thought on this for an hour or two and then came back with some better thoughts once my emotions settle down?"

That is good and godly.

But that is not what I was doing, nor is it what many other men are doing when they are silent with their spouses.

Just yesterday, I watched one of our children purposely not respond to their sibling because they were angry with them. It caused the other child a great deal of frustration as she was trying to use her words to process her emotions but couldn't get a response.

Fighting poorly is sinful and will only cause massive friction within a marriage. Getting loud and aggressive is not fighting well. Neither is being silent or purposefully passive.

I think back to those early days of marriage and still can't believe Leila didn't leave me. She had every right to, but instead, she stayed.

It was her staying that gave me the clearest picture of the gospel I had ever seen. She knew me fully and had seen me at my worst. She could have seen me in those days and said, "I see all of who you are, and as a result, I'm leaving." But she did the opposite.

Her actions said to me, "I see all of who you are, and I love you fully. Not only am I not leaving you, I want to stay and work with God to see you become the man he desires you to be."

> **God sees you fully and loves you fully, so you can do the same for your wife.**

This is the purpose of our marriage: to point each other and the world around us back to that gospel truth.

God sees you fully and loves you fully, so you can do the same for your wife.

The truth is, if you and your wife are experiencing conflict (and who isn't?), you can at least take comfort in knowing that you're not the only ones. Humans have literally had friction in relationships from the very first pages of the Scriptures. We are born sinners and, by default, are prone to our own sinful desires and selfishness. If you put two humans in the same room for any length of time, there is bound to be some kind of friction.

- "Just as sin came into the world through one man, and death through sin, and so death spread to all men because all sinned" (Romans 5:12).

- "The wicked are estranged from the womb;
  they go astray from birth, speaking lies" (Psalm 58:3).

- "You were dead in the trespasses and sins in which you once walked, following the course of this world, following the prince of the power of the air, the spirit that is now at work in the sons of disobedience—among whom we all once lived in the passions of our flesh, carrying out the desires of the body and the mind, and were by nature children of wrath, like the rest of mankind" (Ephesians 2:1-3).

Sin isn't just what we do. It's in our very nature. And as long as there are sinful people, there will be friction in relationships.

> **Sin isn't just what we do. It's in our very nature.**

This is why we sell our children short when we instruct them to simply "stop fighting." Sure, maybe they'll stop bickering for a minute, or maybe even a few days, but human friction will always be part of their life experiences. True discipleship involves teaching our children not simply how to avoid conflict but rather how to handle it in a God-honoring way.

If you were to read the Bible from cover to cover, you wouldn't get the impression that God thinks there will be no fighting among humans. In fact,

True discipleship involves teaching our children not simply how to avoid conflict but rather how to handle it in a God-honoring way.

Q&A MIXTAPE

quite the contrary. The Scriptures are clear that relational friction will be part of the human story in a broken world, and therefore, God provides wisdom as to how his people are to respond.

Look at what James says in the first chapter of his letter:

> Know this, my beloved brothers: let every person be quick to hear, slow to speak, slow to anger; for the anger of man does not produce the righteousness of God. Therefore put away all filthiness and rampant wickedness and receive with meekness the implanted word, which is able to save your souls (James 1:19-21).

> **As long as there are broken and sinful people on this earth, we need tools to handle conflict in godly ways.**

Why would someone need to be quick to hear, slow to speak, and slow to anger? Well, because as sinful humans, we are prone to want to get angry with others quickly, demand that they agree with our perspectives, and not listen to what they are trying to say. James is not saying that people won't experience relational friction; instead, he's telling them how to act when they inevitably do.

A day is coming when God will make all things new. Our hearts long to live in a world where there is no more pain, suffering, or evil. But for now, as long as there are broken and sinful people on this earth, we need tools to handle conflict in godly ways.

Like James, the book of Luke also provides tactics on how to honor God amid friction. Check this out:

> If your brother sins, rebuke him, and if he repents, forgive him, and if he sins against you seven times in the day, and turns to you seven times, saying, "I repent," you must forgive him (Luke 17:3-4).

Again, the writers of the Scriptures knew that people would sin against one another. The game plan wasn't to tell the disciples to simply knock it off but to train their hearts toward godliness in the midst of a broken world.

Finally, look at this verse in Ephesians 4:

> Be angry and do not sin; do not let the sun go down on your anger (Ephesians 4:26).

I honestly can't imagine how my life would have been different if I were taught these things when I was a child and how much they would have helped me as a young married man. I was told not to fight instead of trained on how to fight well, and in a way that honors the Lord. Perhaps that was your experience too.

I remember standing at the kitchen sink, shirt wet from the water that had been splashing me as I washed the dishes, and feeling that the Holy Spirit had been graciously parenting my heart in that moment. He took all of what had just happened—me yelling at my children, getting a text from a Dad Tired member, and the remembrance of the Scriptures—and used it all to start connecting the dots.

I walked up the stairs and asked my kids to sit down on the couch with me. I knew I needed to use this moment to parent their hearts the same way God had just parented mine.

As we sat on the couch together, I began to repent and apologize for the way I had yelled at them moments before.

"Listen. Daddy didn't grow up learning how to fight well," I started. "When Mommy and I got married, I was a bad fighter. I used to yell and say mean things, a lot like the way you guys sometimes argue with one another.

I don't want you to grow up and get married one day without knowing how to fight well.

"Mommy and I fight—we disagree on things—but we have learned how to fight well. That's what I want for you. I want you to learn how to fight well. And I'm sorry that I haven't taken the time to teach you guys how to fight better. From now on, my promise to you as your daddy is to teach you how to fight in a way that honors God."

At first, my kids looked at me almost as if I was joking.

> **As the spiritual leaders of our home, we must be fathers who take the time to parent our children's hearts, not just manage their behavior.**

"Wait, you're going to just let us fight?" my eight-year-old daughter asked.

"Yes, I am. Because conflict will always be part of your life. But I will step in if I hear that you aren't fighting well and in a way that honors Jesus."

"Whoa," my son said quietly, as he tried to wrap his head around this new reality.

We spent the next fifteen minutes talking about all the ways a person who loves Jesus can fight well. We compiled a list, wrote it down on a piece of paper, and hung it up on the refrigerator to use as a reference during our next family conflict.

Here's the reality: One day, our sons and daughters may be husbands and wives. And when that day comes, they'll likely be fighting over things with much larger consequences than who should share the yellow LEGOs. As the spiritual leaders of our home, we must be fathers who take the time to parent our children's hearts, not just manage their behavior. We must shepherd and train them the same way God shepherds and trains us. We must prepare them for a world, work environments, and marriages that will have conflict. And we must teach them not to run from it but to face it head-on with grace, patience, and God-honoring peace.

OUR SEVEN FAMILY RULES FOR FIGHTING

Here is a list of rules we have for fighting well in our family. Feel free to steal any that make sense for you and your family or add others as you'd like.

1. *Be a good listener.* As followers of Jesus, we want to be disciples who are slow to speak, quick to listen, and slow to anger.

2. *Watch your tone.* How you say something is just as important as what you say. Good fighters know what to say to bring peace, but also how to say it.

3. *Ask for a short break.* It's okay if you're emotions are getting the best of you and you just need a minute to calm down, reset, and then come back to resolve the issue. The caveat is, this break has to be around thirty minutes to an hour, and it can't last for days. This is not an excuse to avoid conflict.[3]

4. *No interrupting.* If you want to learn how to fight well, you must be a good listener. Each person should have the opportunity to share their full thoughts without being interrupted.

5. *Name your emotion.* This is a rule we cover a lot in our Family Leadership Program during the marriage portion of our training. It's incredibly helpful in both marriage and parenting. Fights tend to be way less explosive, and much shorter, when all parties

---

3. This is a great rule for marriage conflict as well.

can name the emotion they are feeling. Examples: "I feel mad. I feel sad. I feel scared. I feel frustrated. I feel hurt." And so on.

6. *Ask good questions.* A good question sounds something like, "Are there specific times where this behavior causes you more frustration?" Or "What can I do to better help next time?" Fighters who honor God are fighters who grow in empathy. Good questions allow the opportunity for empathy to grow.

7. *Tell the truth and don't blame.* A family that honors God in the midst of conflict is a family who becomes fluent in truth-telling. They are not afraid of the truth, and they are not afraid of owning their own mistakes. We must raise truth-tellers who are quick to repent.

QUESTIONS TO CONSIDER

1. When you look back on your own marriage, would you consider yourself a God-honoring fighter?

2. What is your go-to behavior when faced with conflict? Do you get loud, quiet, passive, or something else?

3. Would you say you were trained on how to fight well as a child? What do you remember being taught about fighting and conflict in your early years?

4. Which of the seven rules of fighting stuck out to you most and why?

5. What would it look like to parent your child's heart instead of their behavior?

6. Using the list of rules above as motivation, write down your own list of rules for your family.

DABBLING MUSICIAN

My Dad Life as a Christian

Sometimes I like to pretend I'm a real musician.

Now, if you know me well, you might think I'm being facetious by saying that. That's because during my late teens and early twenties, I played drums professionally in a band. My first position in vocational ministry was as a worship pastor for a large church. Music has always been a big part of my life.

In fact, my dad is a professional musician to this day. He has made a living performing in front of crowds since he was sixteen—more than fifty years of music! Even though he wasn't around much when I was a kid, I still feel like that musical DNA just kind of seeped its way into my blood.

But honestly, I'm not a real musician; I know just enough to be dangerous. I can fake it around some people who don't know anything about music, but a real musician would spot me as an imposter from a mile away.

True story: On my very first Sunday of leading the music as a worship pastor in front of nearly 2,000 people, I took one strum of the guitar before the strap broke. The guitar immediately crashed to the ground and landed at my feet. I stood in shock as the band stopped playing behind me. I slowly looked down at the broken guitar and then back up at the congregation, who were staring at me in awkward silence. I felt like my pants had just fallen down, and I can assure you it was as embarrassing as you can picture it being in your head.

I'm not a real musician; I'm just good at faking it. I can dabble around on an old guitar and might be able to make it sound good from time to time. But put me in a room full of real musicians, and you'll quickly discover that I can't keep up.

Sometimes I wonder how many of our churches are filled with men who know just enough about Jesus to be dangerous but aren't quite the real thing. I know that might sound harsh, but hear me out.

> **Jesus followers were never meant to dabble on Christianity from time to time but instead were meant to be all-consumed.**

I've had to ask myself on more than one occasion, *Am I a real Jesus follower, or am I just good at faking it?*

I mean, come on. My mom and grandma were Christians. Doesn't that Christian DNA just kind of get passed down from generation to generation? Doesn't their faith automatically seep into my blood?

Here's where things get real convicting for me: when I'm standing in a room with real Jesus followers who are taking their role as Christians seriously. They aren't simply dabbling in the things of God; they are instead living and breathing the gospel with every ounce of their being. I start to wonder if they can spot an imposter from a mile away.

Real musicians don't dabble on a guitar from time to time. They are consumed by it.

I wonder if real Jesus followers were never meant to dabble on Christianity from time to time but instead were meant to be all-consumed.

When I read the words of Jesus in the Gospels, I don't really get the sense that he was calling people to dabble or to fake it till they made it.

> If anyone would come after me, let him deny himself and take up his cross daily and follow me. For whoever would save his life will lose it, but whoever loses his life for my sake will save it. For what does it profit a man if he gains the whole world and loses or forfeits himself? For whoever is ashamed of me and of my words, of him will the Son of Man be ashamed when he comes in his glory and the glory of the Father and of the holy angels. But I tell you truly, there are some standing here who will not taste death until they see the kingdom of God (Luke 9:23-27).

> Now great crowds accompanied him, and he turned and said to them, "If anyone comes to me and does not hate his own father and mother and wife and children and brothers and sisters, yes, and even his own life, he cannot be my disciple. Whoever does not bear his own cross and come after me cannot be my disciple. For which of you, desiring to build a tower, does not first sit down and count the cost, whether he has enough to complete it? Otherwise, when he has laid a foundation and is not able to finish, all who see it begin to mock him, saying, 'This man began to build and was not able to finish.' Or what king, going out to encounter another king in war, will not sit down first and deliberate whether he is able with ten thousand to meet him who comes against him with twenty thousand? And if not, while the other is yet a great way off, he sends a delegation and asks for terms of peace. So therefore, any one of you who does not renounce all that he has cannot be my disciple" (Luke 14:25-33).

As you read those words from Jesus, do you get the sense that he was calling people to dabble in the things of God? Quite the opposite.

Imagine Beethoven walking into the room right now and saying, "I'm

Are you just dabbling in this whole
God thing, or are you willing to give
up your life to change the world?

Q&A MIXTAPE

going to teach you how to play incredible music—music so good, it will change the world."

You'd probably respond with something like, "Wow—that's amazing! What's it going to cost me?"

"Your life," he responds in a serious tone.

"My life?"

"Yes. You're going to have to give up everything. The life you currently know will no longer exist. You will spend your entire life devoted to learning this music. But if you do, it will change the world."

At that point, you'd have to ask yourself, *Am I really all in? Do I actually want to do this, or do I simply just want to make an old guitar sound cool from time to time?*

When Jesus called his disciples, he invited them to leave behind everything they had known up until that point. He called them to give up their lives to change the world.

Why am I telling you all this?

Brother, before you read one more chapter of this book, I want you to ask yourself honestly: Are you all in, or are you simply trying to learn enough about Jesus to make an old guitar sound cool from time to time?

I know that doesn't make sense, but you know what I mean, right? Are you just dabbling in this whole God thing, or are you willing to give up your life to change the world?

Have you convinced yourself that you need just enough Jesus to raise some good kids, have a nice marriage, and be a good person? Or have you counted the cost of what it means to truly be his disciple?

I want you to pause right now. There is literally nothing more important in the world at this moment than honestly asking yourself this question: *Am I all in?*

It's going to cost you your life. But if you say yes, Jesus will make you new from the inside out. He will teach you a way of living that will change you, your family, your community, and the world around you for generations to come.

I'm just a guy who can play a guitar a little; I'm not a real musician. Real musicians are consumed by music.

> **Let's not be dads who just sprinkle in some Jesus from time to time.**

Let's not be dads who just sprinkle in some Jesus from time to time. Those aren't real Jesus followers. A true disciple soberly counts the cost. He takes the time to recognize what this will require from him. There will be habits he needs to address. Sins he needs to bring to the light to confess. Addictions that need healing. Routines that need to be altered.

It will cost you your life, brother. But if you are willing to take the narrow road, everything around you will change.

Your life as a Christian dad doesn't involve picking up a guitar from time to time. Your family needs more than that. They need a husband and dad who is all in. They need a man leading them toward change as he himself is being changed by the gospel from the inside out.

Don't skip this part.

Are you all in?

QUESTIONS TO CONSIDER

1. As you reflect on your life, what made you decide to follow Jesus? Did you ever make that conscious decision, or did you subtly assume you're a Christian because other people in your family are?

2. What does counting the cost look like for you? What would you need to sacrifice in order to truly follow Jesus with everything you have?

3. If you're a Christian, would you say you've dabbled in the things of Jesus, or have you been all in? Do you know anyone who seems like they are all in for Christ? If so, how does their life look different from yours?

P13X

How Can I Pursue My Relationship with God? (Spiritual Disciplines)

I grew up playing sports from the time I was a young boy all the way through high school. I did it partly because I loved the competition, but also because it was a great way for me to try to stay active without having to go to the gym.[1] After I graduated high school, though, I found myself quickly putting on the notorious "freshman fifteen." Except my fifteen was more like twenty to thirty extra pounds of unnecessary weight. After about six months of sitting around and being lazy, I decided it was finally time to lose my pre–dad bod figure. That's when I searched online for at-home workout programs and discovered the newly released program called P90X. It was all the rage. You could pop a disc into the DVD player and spend forty-five minutes with a chiseled personal trainer yelling at you to finish your set of push-ups, all within the comfort of your own living room.

It was honestly amazing, and I was immediately hooked. In fact, I did the program probably thirteen times.

---

1. If you read my book *Dad Tired and Loving It*, you know I don't have good experiences at gyms.

Okay, I should rephrase that. I *started* the program about thirteen times. I never finished. Not once did I get to day ninety. I don't even know what workouts came past day thirteen because that's usually where I called it quits.

I guess you could say I'm more of a P13X kind of guy.

The truth is, I'm not super disciplined. I get really into things for a very short amount of time and then can never seem to stick with them until the end. Leila has never come right out and said it to me directly, but I'm convinced she likely hates this part of my personality. The hobbies I've taken up and never finished have left me with a garage full of dusty junk that will likely be sold for pennies at our next garage sale.

I have some friends who are ridiculously disciplined. They set routines and stick with them like robots.

Not me. When I start a one-year Bible reading plan, I'm already behind on day two.

What about you? Where do you fall on that spectrum? Are you crazy disciplined, or do you find yourself setting goals that you never quite achieve?

> **Spiritual disciplines are a gift for you as a son of God. They are not a prerequisite for his love.**

As Christians, we know how important it is to have regular spiritual disciplines that keep our hearts pointed toward Jesus. And yet most of us feel like we can never quite keep up with them. We know we should be reading the Bible more, praying more, and so on, but our behavior rarely lines up with our heart's motivation.

If you find yourself closer to the "falling behind on day two" side of the discipline spectrum, take heart; God's love for you does not waver based on how disciplined you are. He isn't angry with you if you're not consistently waking up at four in the morning to spend an hour in prayer before the family gets up to start the day.

Spiritual disciplines are a gift for you as a son of God. They are not a prerequisite for his love.

Becoming more disciplined will not make God love you more. It won't even make you a better Christian—there's no such thing. But it will offer you a closer relationship with your heavenly Father. And the more time you spend with Jesus, the more like him you start to become. As you draw near to Jesus, you start to act more like him, talk more like him, and even love more like him.

> As you draw near to Jesus, you start to act more like him, talk more like him, and even love more like him.

His presence is a gift for your good, not a checklist to be mastered.

I'm going to spend the rest of this chapter sharing some of my favorite spiritual disciplines. I'll be totally honest from the jump; I'm never good at all of these at the same time. Depending on the season of life I'm in, and how many babies I have waking up in the middle of the night, I'm really just focusing on one or two at a time. In some seasons of life, I may be crushing it at my morning routine but neglecting to fast, or spend time in silence, or vice versa.

I'd suggest picking one of these that you are not currently doing and practicing it for four weeks straight. If you can, spend a couple minutes journaling your experience as you go through the daily exercise. My guess is that after four weeks, you'll start to feel like this is more of a habit and less of a chore. You'll likely realize the gift of God's presence that you've been missing out on all along.

THE PRACTICE OF SILENCE

A few years back, Leila and I moved the family from the Portland suburbs to a small country town about forty-five minutes from the city. Our goal was to give the kids a little more space to roam and play out in the beautiful Oregon countryside.

I'll never forget the very first night we stayed in the new house. Leila and I were lying in bed, exhausted after a long day of moving and unpacking what felt like a never-ending pile of boxes. After spending a couple minutes talking about our game plan for the next day, we quickly laid our heads down on the pillows to fall asleep.

About five minutes passed by before Leila turned to me and said, "Babe, you still awake?"

"Yep. Wide awake." We both started to laugh.

"Why it is so stinkin' quiet in here?" she asked.

"I guess this is country life."

We weren't used to going to bed in such a quiet house. We had spent our whole marriage living in homes surrounded by noise coming from outside traffic, neighbors, sirens, and all kinds of other disruptions. In fact, the constant noise had almost become soothing to us. It was such a part of our subconscious that when it disappeared, it was distracting.

> **For most of us, silence can be distracting.**

The silence literally kept us awake.

We were so thrown off by the lack of noise that we actually had to download sound machine apps on our phones that would allow us to fill our bedroom with synthetic white noise, just to fall asleep.

For most of us, silence can be distracting. For some, it's terrifying. Silence has a way of immediately pushing to the surface whatever our subconscious was working so hard to keep buried down deep within our souls.

But here's the amazing thing: Healing will often use the path of silence to break through the forest of noise that our souls so often find themselves lost in.

I want you to ask yourself something right now: Is there a situation you're currently faced with that you need the wisdom of the Holy Spirit to guide you through? If so, what is your plan to hear the voice of God? You may be quietly and desperately asking God to show up for you and to give you an answer, but have you given him the space to speak to your soul?

God rarely shouts, but in my experience, his voice seems to be loudest in the quiet places.

If you're like me, your life is likely filled with all kinds of noise: work, advertisements, TV, social media, apps, news stories, and probably the actual noise of your busy household. In fact, I wouldn't be surprised if you were interrupted while trying to read this book.

Everything is trying to speak to your soul, but there is only One who can fill it. There's a reason Jesus got away to quiet places to be with the Father.

> God rarely shouts, but in my experience, his voice seems to be loudest in the quiet places.

Rising very early in the morning, while it was still dark, he departed and went out to a desolate place, and there he prayed (Mark 1:35).

What would it look like for you to "depart to a desolate place" and spend some time with the Lord, seeking his voice, his wisdom, and his presence?

Listen, I'm not naive enough to think that as a busy man, you're able to just break away and go spend some alone time in the woods somewhere for

What would it look like for you to "depart to a desolate place" and spend some time with the Lord, seeking his voice, his wisdom, and his presence?

Q&A MIXTAPE

a few days. You likely have a busy life and family to manage. But how could you break away regularly to spend some time with Jesus?

For me, it means taking a ten- to fifteen-minute lunch break outside every day (or as often as possible each week). I keep my phone inside, go sit out on the patio, and just sit in silence. I don't pray any long, fancy prayers. I don't expect the sky to open up or the clouds to write some magical words that will somehow make sense to me. I just sit quietly and ask God to speak to me. Sometimes there is clarity on something my soul has been subconsciously wrestling with. But honestly, most times, it's just a refreshing break from the bombardment of distractions trying to fill my eyes, ears, heart, and mind.

> **We long for God to speak to us but don't always give him a chance.**

We long for God to speak to us but don't always give him a chance.

As the spiritual leaders of our homes, we must take the time needed to allow God to speak to our souls. It's hard to lead a family when you have no idea what God is trying to say.

Pull out your calendar right now and block out three fifteen-minute times when you can practice sitting in silence. During those times, ask God to speak to you and to give you the wisdom you are longing for.

THE PRACTICE OF PURGING

While I was unloading the groceries into the house today, I was quietly singing this line repeatedly: "I've got those moves like Jagger, got those moves like Jagger…"

As I finished putting the squeezable apple sauce pouches into the refrigerator, I turned around to see Leila staring at me with a blank stare on her face.

"What's up?" I asked, unable to get a read on her body language.

"Well, babe. You've been letting the whole house know that you have 'moves like Jagger' for the last ten minutes."

"What are you talking about?" I asked, confused. "I've just been putting away the groceries."

"Yeah, and while you've been doing that, you've also been singing 'Moves like Jagger' and shaking your backside around the whole kitchen."

"Are you serious?" I was genuinely confused.

I hadn't noticed that the song was running in the back of my mind, and I especially didn't realize I had been singing it for the last several minutes. I concluded that the song must have been playing on the radio during my drive home and that it had been subconsciously stuck in my head.

The brain has a crazy way of holding on to things, oftentimes without us even realizing it.

If you've ever moved into a new-to-you home, like Leila and I did, you were likely surprised by the number of things you had collected over the years. I've moved nearly a dozen times, and yet I still trick myself into thinking that I don't have as much stuff as I really do.

During our last move, I had asked some friends to help me load the moving truck.

"Sure, man, I'll help you guys out," one buddy responded when I asked him if he could spare an hour or two to help pack things up.

"Sweet, I appreciate that. It shouldn't take long; we don't have much," I told him, completely naive to the amount of junk I had stored up over the years.

What I imagined would be a one- or two-hour project turned into multiple days of packing and moving.

I want you to pause for a minute and imagine your brain as a house. How many things do you think you've collected in there over the years? Does it feel nice and tidy, or is it full of unwanted items? If you're like me, my guess is you have a lot more junk stored up than you'd like to admit.

Our brains are sticky. They have a way of collecting, boxing up, and keeping around all the things we let in. Even the stuff we hope wouldn't stick around.

So what does this mean for you as the spiritual leader of your home?

It means that if you're serious about leading your family well and becoming the man God is calling you to be, you must be serious about what you let into your "house." What may feel small, insignificant, or inconsequential now will likely turn into a garage so packed full of stuff that you can't find the door.

> **Pause for a minute and imagine your brain as a house. How many things do you think you've collected in there over the years?**

Let me try to make this analogy a little more real. Think about the last forty-eight hours of your life. What things have you let into your eyes and ears that you convinced yourself aren't really a big deal?

Did you look at porn?

Did you watch a show filled with violence, vulgarity, or something else explicit?

Did you listen to music or a podcast that made you feel anger toward people? Objectify women? Or feel hopeless about our world?

I'm not trying to shame you, trust me. I'd be embarrassed if you saw all the things I willingly let into my own eyes and ears.

My point is, those things don't just enter our brains and then get thrown out. We can't be that naive. Instead, they stick. They get packed up and stored away somewhere deep in our brains and souls. It may have felt inno-cent or insignificant at the time, but now we look around, and our house is full of junk. It sticks around.

Let me put it a little more directly: You are being shaped by the things you are watching and listening to.

> You are being shaped by the things you are watching and listening to.

Most of us don't want to believe that reality. We'd like to convince ourselves that we are inde-pendent men, free from the influences of the outside world.

Brother, don't be deceived. What you watch and what you listen to are changing you as a man. They are shaping your heart. They change the way you interact with your wife, your kids, and the world around you.

Listen to what the writer says in Philippians 4:

> Finally, brothers, whatever is true, whatever is honorable, whatever is just, whatever is pure, whatever is lovely, whatever is commend-able, if there is any excellence, if there is anything worthy of praise, think about these things (Philippians 4:8).

Or how about this verse in Joshua:

> This Book of the Law shall not depart from your mouth, but you shall meditate on it day and night, so that you may be careful to do according to all that is written in it (Joshua 1:8).

Again, I want you to think about the last forty-eight hours of your life. How many things did you meditate on that were pure, lovely, and com-mendable? Were the things that you willingly let into your eyes and ears "worthy of praise"?

As the spiritual leaders of our homes, I'm convinced that the more junk we let into our "houses," the messier our actual households become.

Take a minute and list out everything that you willingly meditate on during a regular week. List the news sources you turn to, the apps you spend the most time on, the shows you watch, the music and podcasts you listen to, and so on. Now take that list and measure it against those two verses from Philippians and Joshua that I listed above. Do they make the cut? Are they pure, lovely, and worthy of praise?

I encourage you to do what many others have done before you in their longing to be more like Christ: Purge the things in your life that do not bring God glory and are not beneficial for your soul or the well-being of your family.

> Purge the things in your life that do not bring God glory and are not beneficial for your soul or the well-being of your family.

Spiritual leaders know that their eyes and ears are not only the gateways to their own souls but also the gateways the enemy often uses to infiltrate the family.

Protect them at all costs.

THE PRACTICE OF CONFESSION

Last week I had the privilege of speaking to a couple hundred men at a men's retreat. I'm not sure there are many things better than being in a room full of humble guys who are seriously trying to figure out who Jesus is and what it looks like to follow him more seriously. I have yet to see God not show up in big ways every time I'm at one of these events.

On the second night of the retreat, I had just finished teaching a message when I saw a man standing off to the side. I could barely get offstage before he walked right up to me. His eyes told me that he was feeling nervous and emotional.

"Hey, Jerrad, thank you for that message. I feel like God is telling me to confess something to you," he said through a shaky voice.

I'll be honest: These moments are always a bit difficult for me. In some ways, I feel like a Catholic priest sitting on the other side of a confessional booth, listening to a stranger pour out his secret sins. I don't believe that Christians are required to confess their sins to clergy, but I'm also open to wherever the Spirit is leading. If this man felt led by God to share something, I don't want to get in the way of his obedience.

"Of course, man. What's going on?" I responded to him.

Those words could barely leave my mouth before he began to weep. Just me giving him the permission to share what was on his heart allowed the floodgates of his soul to burst open wide. He sobbed for several minutes while I put my hand on his shoulder.

"It's okay, bro. God can handle your worst. There's grace for you, even on your worst day," I calmly reminded him.

It took nearly ten minutes for him to control his tears well enough to begin speaking. As he composed himself, he began sharing some extremely deep and painful experiences from his childhood. He confessed that he had never shared these things with anyone else before now.

"I've asked God a million times for forgiveness, but I still carry around such a big weight on my shoulders," he said, continuing to cry.

I could almost feel the overwhelmingly heavy sense of guilt and shame that this man had been carrying around for nearly his entire life. I spent the next several minutes praying with him and reminding him of who Jesus says he is through the gospel.

We ended our conversation with a hug, and he headed back to his cabin

for the night. The next morning, I saw him in line at breakfast and immediately went over to say hi.

"Good morning, bro!"

He was smiling from ear to ear. I kid you not, he literally looked different.
I know that sounds weird and a bit supernatural, but I was truly taken aback
by the difference in his overall demeanor just hours after the last time I had
talked with him. I don't know how else to describe it other than comparing
the look of a guy who had been carrying around a bag of rocks in the desert
for several miles to the look of a guy who got a full night's rest and looked
totally refreshed. The guy I had talked to the night before looked exhausted.
The man I saw in the morning looked like he had a newly refreshed soul.

He had the look of someone who had been healed.

I wonder if you're thinking, *Man, I want a renewed soul too. I need that
same kind of healing.*

I'd be foolish to think that my new friend at the conference is the only
guy carrying around a heavy bag of rocks. You, too, may be deeply burdened
by the weight of your own sin and shame. Maybe you have asked God a million times to forgive you and to take this pain away from you, and yet you
still feel like you are weighed down from your past or present sins.

I have some good news for you, man. Look at this verse in 1 John:

> If we confess our sins, he is faithful and just to forgive us our sins and
> to cleanse us from all unrighteousness (1 John 1:9).

If you have truly confessed your sins to God, you are forgiven. Period.
Whether or not you feel forgiven doesn't change reality; he *has* forgiven you,
and you *are* cleansed from unrighteousness.

If you have confessed, you have been forgiven. Forgiveness is not the issue for you; healing is. You have been forgiven, but you have yet to be healed.

Q&A MIXTAPE

Now, I know what you're thinking: *That's nice, Jerrad. But it doesn't change the fact that I walk around with this heavy burden all the time. I know God forgives me, but I certainly don't feel forgiven.*

If you relate to that thought, I have more good news. Look at what Jesus's brother James says his New Testament letter:

> Therefore, confess your sins to one another and pray for one another, that you may be healed. The prayer of a righteous person has great power as it is working (James 5:16).

If you have confessed, you have been forgiven. Forgiveness is not the issue for you; healing is. You have been forgiven, but you have yet to be healed.

Healing is what that man experienced at the conference that night. He confessed his sins to another brother, and as a result, God gave him the miraculous gift of healing.

Confession to God brings forgiveness. Confession to one another brings healing.

Here's the truth, man: Satan's favorite playground is the one he's built in your head. He has convinced you (and many others like you) that your sin is unmanageable. He's the father of lies.

Confession to God brings forgiveness. Confession to one another brings healing.

> He was a murderer from the beginning, and does not stand in the truth, because there is no truth in him. When he lies, he speaks out of his own character, for he is a liar and the father of lies (John 8:44).

His tactics are always the same. First, he lies by telling you that your sin will satisfy your soul more than Jesus can. And then, once you believe that lie and fall into temptation, he convinces you that because of your sin, you are now hopeless. He plays that track on repeat in the darkness of your mind.

But as always, he's a liar.

You aren't hopeless, because Jesus made a way.

> Spiritual leadership must involve two things: regular confession of sin to God and regular confession of sin to one another.

This is the power of confessing to another brother. You turn the lights on. You expose Satan for what he is: a liar. You give another believer the opportunity to remind you that you're being lied to, and more importantly, the opportunity to remind you of gospel truth: that your worth is based not on what you've done but on what's been done for you by Jesus Christ.

Spiritual leadership must involve two things: regular confession of sin to God and regular confession of sin to one another.

This is how we continue to walk in healing as men. This is how we keep the lights on in the playground and remind the enemy that he's not allowed to play there.

One of the hardest yet most powerful spiritual disciplines you can practice as a man is to find another brother and meet regularly to confess your sins and weaknesses and then spend time praying for each other.

THE PRACTICE OF SABBATH

I'm writing this chapter from the middle seat of an airplane. The guy next to me just took his shoes off and seems to be oblivious to the fact that his feet most certainly do not smell like roses. He also doesn't seem to understand that the armrest is designed for the both of us. Three of my kids are sitting directly behind me. My two-year-old tried to stand up and walk around the plane during takeoff, causing a flight attendant to nearly have a heart attack. My eight- and ten-year-olds just told me how hungry they are despite the fact that I bought them some pizza about thirty minutes before we got onto the flight. I just looked over at Leila, who is holding our fussy one-year-old daughter on her lap; she looks as stressed as I am.

This family vacation is exhausting.

Each year we decide not to give Christmas gifts and instead to take a family vacation together. Our goal is to create memories rather than fill the house with plastic toys that undoubtedly will be thrown away or donated just months later.

At this point, I think some plastic toys would have been easier. I have spent the week hauling luggage around like a pack mule, losing endless nights of sleep in hotel rooms, and stressing about the amount of money we're spending for food my kids never finish.

The phrase "I need a vacation from my vacation" has never felt more relatable.

You know the crazy part? I had been looking forward to this trip for months because I kept telling myself how nice it will be to finally get away and get some rest. I convinced myself that pulling away from the chaos of our day-to-day lives and spending a week in a sunny destination would finally give me the much-needed rest my body and soul so desperately longed for.

I think I miscalculated. I feel more exhausted than ever.

When was the last time you felt well-rested? I don't just mean you had a good night's rest, but rather than you felt a deep sense of peace. The kind of peace that encompasses your body, mind, and soul.

I think most of us are convinced that if we can just get a few more things done, we'll finally feel a little more rested. How many times have you heard someone say, "It's just a crazy season of life right now, but when things settle down..."?

Have you ever heard that? Maybe you're the one who is saying it.

My next question would be, Have things settled down yet, or are you still waiting for that day to come?

We have a funny way of trying to pack in rest. Each day we work long hours and then try to run on as little sleep as possible. We work for months or years on end and then try to squeeze in a week or two of vacation, hoping to refill our tanks.

How's that working? Do you feel rested?

Do you remember the creation story back in Genesis? God spends six days speaking all of creation into existence. On the sixth day, he creates his most prized possession: humans.

> Then God said, "Let us make man in our image, after our likeness. And let them have dominion over the fish of the sea and over the birds of the heavens and over the livestock and over all the earth and over every creeping thing that creeps on the earth."
>
> So God created man in his own image,
> in the image of God he created him;
> male and female he created them.
>
> And God saw everything that he had made, and behold, it was very good. And there was evening and there was morning, the sixth day (Genesis 1:26-27,31).

God spends six days creating, and then he steps back and sees that it is very good. He takes pride in his workmanship. Check out what happens right after:

Thus the heavens and the earth were finished, and all the host of them. And on the seventh day God finished his work that he had done, and he rested on the seventh day from all his work that he had done. So God blessed the seventh day and made it holy, because on it God rested from all his work that he had done in creation (Genesis 2:1-3).

Now, what's crazy about this portion of the Scripture is not just the fact that God took a day to rest but that his very first day with humans is a rest day. He creates humans and then commissions them to work and to fill the earth. But first, they rest. It's almost as if he wanted the humans to know that before they accomplish anything, they must first just spend some time with the Father.

Man. Let that truth sink in for a minute.

What if before God wants you to do anything else this week, he first just wants you to spend time with him, accomplishing nothing other than being loved as his son?

What would your typical week look like if you started it by spending a day remembering that before you're a dad, a husband, or a worker, you're first a beloved son of the Most High?

There are loads of great books covering the topic of Sabbath. In fact, we've had several authors on our show talking about the subject in depth.[2] But let me just boil it all down to this very simple truth: It's extremely hard to be the spiritual leader of your home if you and your family are always exhausted.

Brother, you must operate out a place of rest instead of constantly trying to seek rest out of your exhaustion. I think this is why Jesus most likely looked at the exhausted people around him and offered them this invitation:

---

2. Search the Dad Tired website for John Mark Comer, A.J. Swoboda, Jeremy Pryor, or Jefferson Bethke.

Come to me, all who labor and are heavy laden, and I will give you rest. Take my yoke upon you, and learn from me, for I am gentle and lowly in heart, and you will find rest for your souls (Matthew 11:28-29).

Rested souls have been part of God's design from day one—literally.

So what does it practically look like to start your week with the spiritual practice of Sabbath? Well, the good news is, there are no rules. This is a gift for you from the Father, not a command full of rules you must obey. Don't overcomplicate it. The main goal here is to help you and your family remember that you can't earn God's love by accomplishing more. Instead, you are reminded that even while you accomplish nothing, you are deeply loved by the Father.

> **You must operate out of a place of rest instead of constantly trying to seek rest out of your exhaustion.**

Here are some tips that will help you get started on your practice of Sabbath. Use it as a template to get your creative juices flowing. Remember, the practice of Sabbath can take months if not years to settle into. Because of sin, we are prone to stay busy in order to feel accomplished, worthy, and valuable. Fighting against that and resting in gospel truth takes a lot of work, but it's worth fighting for.

- Block out four days over the next month that you can spend together as a family. Remember, the day is not as important as the practice itself. Our family typically practices Sabbath on Saturdays, but that changes from time to time depending on our schedule.

- Ask each person in the family what gives them rest. For my wife, sitting in a coffee shop alone drinking a hot beverage absolutely fills her tank. To me, it sounds like torture. I like to mow the lawn

and use my hands outside. Ask each person in the family to name
something they enjoy doing that they don't normally get to do.

- Eat dinner around the table together. We like to use special
  plates reserved only for our Sabbath dinner. We also make sure
  there is no technology at the table and even use candles to light
  the room. This helps the kids remember that Sabbath is different
  and set apart from every other day.

- Pick one activity you can all do together that you normally
  wouldn't have a chance to do during the week. Some ideas
  include going on a family walk, watching a movie together,
  doing a puzzle, playing in the yard, cooking a meal or dessert
  together, and so on.

Remember, don't overcomplicate it or give
up after a few awkward tries. The truth is this:
Your soul doesn't need another vacation, another
lazy day on the couch, or a getaway with the
boys. Your soul needs to be constantly reminded
that you are loved despite what you can accomplish. I pray that as you start to practice the discipline of Sabbath, your soul begins to find the
deep rest that Jesus longs for you to experience
in him.

> **Your soul needs to be constantly reminded that you are loved despite what you can accomplish.**

For a much more in-depth look at the subject of Sabbath, head to
dadtired.com/rest.

THE PRACTICE OF READING THE SCRIPTURES

My next-door neighbors have a tree that has fallen onto our house three times. I wish I were kidding. The tree is completely dead, and one by one, its massive branches break off and land on our roof. They're lucky I serve a master who commands me to love my neighbor; otherwise, I would have already been over there with a chainsaw.

Take a look at this verse from Psalm 1 about trees:

> Blessed is the man
>   who walks not in the counsel of the wicked,
> nor stands in the way of sinners,
>   nor sits in the seat of scoffers;
> but his delight is in the law of the LORD,
>   and on his law he meditates day and night.
> He is like a tree
>   planted by streams of water
> that yields its fruit in its season,
>   and its leaf does not wither.
> In all that he does, he prospers.

The wicked are not so,
but are like chaff that the wind drives away (Psalm 1:1-4).

Here's the thing about dead trees: They're not hard to spot. They are often withered, broken, and falling apart.

I wonder if the same can be said for the man not planted near the living water of Jesus. Often he, too, is exhausted, broken, and searching for satisfaction in all the wrong places. His soul is looking for water in the middle of the desert.

As you evaluate where you're at in life right now, would you say you're like a tree planted near living water or a tree barely hanging on? If you're closer to the latter of those options, I have some good news for you: You don't need to overcomplicate things or overspiritualize things. Simply come back to the water. Plant yourself near the streams as you meditate on the Scriptures day and night.

> **When we study the Scriptures, we are studying the person of God, not a subject to be mastered.**

For those of us who have grown up in and around the church, we can often fall into the trap of subtly convincing ourselves that we know everything we need to know about God in order to live a good Christian life. We've memorized the stories, know all the characters, and maybe have even heard a few hundred sermons presenting different angles on passages we've heard a million times.

But the truth is this: When we study the Scriptures, we are studying the person of God, not a subject to be mastered. We can't have God figured out in the same way we can't have our wives or kids figured out. He's a person, not a subject. He is complex, mysterious, and too massive to wrap our brains around.

And just like when you pursue your wife to grow in intimacy with her, our intimacy with Christ also grows when we pursue getting to know him. In short, he fills our tank in only the ways that he can.

The opposite is also true: When we don't spend time to get to know who God is through his Word, we find ourselves making assumptions about who we'd like him to be. Oftentimes, these assumptions are nowhere near the truth. We're all susceptible to this trap. When we spend time away from the Word of God, our god starts to look more like us and less like the God of the Bible.

Brother, I can assure you that your soul is searching for water from somewhere. It is trying hard to stay hydrated and remain alive. But the truth is, unless you are near the deep well that is the Word of God and are allowing the truth of his Word to fill you up, your soul is most certainly thirsty.

Come back to the only well that can satisfy you. If you miss this spiritual discipline, the rest will be pointless.

QUESTIONS TO CONSIDER

1. When you look at your own spiritual journey, how would you evaluate your spiritual disciplines? Do you have regular spiritual routines, or are you more of a "get behind on day two" kind of guy?

2. Which of the disciplines listed in chapter 8 and this bonus track stuck out to you the most? Is there one in particular you aren't currently doing that you can try to implement into your regular routine?

3. What is one thing in your life that needs to be purged? How much time is that particular thing adding to your calendar each week? What spiritual practice could you replace that time with?

RUNNERS AND WAITERS

How to Make Big and Difficult Decisions as a Family

July 4, 2018, will be a date forever burned into my memory.

I vividly remember sitting on the edge of the sidewalk, waiting for the fireworks to start. In my lap was the three-year-old little girl whom we had been fostering. On the very first day she came into our home, she called me Daddy. That word absolutely broke my heart because I immediately knew how confused this precious little girl was. In her three short years of life, she had already been moved to several homes where strangers attempted to raise her. She had been with us several months before this day of celebration, and it hadn't taken her long to completely steal my heart.

The sun finally set beneath the horizon as neighborhood fireworks began to fill the dark orange summer sky.

"Boom!" one blast after the other rang out, dimming the sounds of cheers and celebration for a few seconds at a time.

After every blast, I could feel her little body sink deeper into my arms as she looked for comfort. She had a beaming smile on her face, but her tense body melting into me indicated that she was looking for safety in me.

Amid the smiles, laughing, and cheers from the crowd, my eyes began to well up with tears.

I love this little girl, I thought.

Until that point, I think there had been a part of me that wasn't ready to fully give in emotionally to the process of foster care. I knew in the back of my mind that she could go home at any point, and I was protecting myself from the pain that would cause by not letting my heart fully invest. But I couldn't hold back any longer.

In that moment, I felt like her dad. She felt like my little girl. The walls my heart had built up came crashing down.

I love this little girl, I said again to myself. *I'm going to adopt her.*

I went to bed that night with a heart full of emotions I had never felt before. I knew God had something big in store, but I had no idea what it would be.

The next morning, everything changed. Her social worker called unexpectedly to let us know that our new little family member would be headed home.

My heart sank.

Actually, scratch that. My heart absolutely broke. So much so, in fact, that I had to excuse myself and go into the other room, where I could finally release the tears that I was so desperately trying to fight back.

Despite knowing that our little girl was going to get to go back home with her mother, who was doing really well, I selfishly wanted her to stay with us forever.

I remember asking God, "Why? Why did you lead us to foster care? Why did I have to become fully emotionally invested literally the day before they would take her home? What is your purpose in all this?"

The decision to become foster parents was long and grueling. Leila and I already had two young kids of our own at home, and we knew it would be difficult to bring in new children to love. We prayed, we fasted, we sought counsel from the Holy Spirit and from our friends, and we ultimately felt like God was calling us to move forward with the decision.

It's weird to type that last sentence, honestly. Even to this day, when someone tells me they feel like God is leading them toward something, I always secretly ask myself, *How do they know for sure God is calling them toward that?* How can we really discern the Lord's leading when it comes to big decisions? Are we really able to tell the differ-ence between the Holy Spirit's prompting and a gassy stomach as a result from lunch?

> **The Scriptures can teach us a lot about how to make big family decisions in wise and biblical ways.**

For us, fostering children was a big decision we had to make. One that we spent months praying about. And even after feeling confident about the Lord's leading, it still wasn't easy. In fact, it was one of the hardest experiences of my life.

What big decision are you currently facing as a family? I know many guys in the Dad Tired community are processing some seriously big life decisions. I've talked to guys who are thinking about switching careers, homeschooling their children, moving to another state, fostering or adopt-ing a child, or some other big life-altering change.

How do you process these big crossroads in your life? Do you just wait to see what happens? Do you list out the "pros" and "cons" of each decision? Do you flip a coin?

Thankfully, I think the Scriptures can teach us a lot about how to make big family decisions in wise and biblical ways. When faced with any major life decision, I often put myself into one of two categories, based on Scrip-ture: runners or waiters. Let me explain.

Take a look at this passage from Luke 9:

> As they were going along the road, someone said to him, "I will fol-
> low you wherever you go." And Jesus said to him, "Foxes have holes,
> and birds of the air have nests, but the Son of Man has nowhere to
> lay his head." To another he said, "Follow me." But he said, "Lord,
> let me first go and bury my father." And Jesus said to him, "Leave
> the dead to bury their own dead. But as for you, go and proclaim
> the kingdom of God." Yet another said, "I will follow you, Lord, but
> let me first say farewell to those at my home." Jesus said to him, "No
> one who puts his hand to the plow and looks back is fit for the king-
> dom of God" (Luke 9:57-62).

When we read this passage of Scripture, we see three people who are
about to make the biggest decision of their lives: the decision to follow Jesus
as one of his disciples. Let's break it down line-by-line, so we can get a better understanding of what's really going on.

> As they were going along the road, someone said to him, "I will fol-
> low you wherever you go."

Here we have Jesus walking down the road when someone appears to
say to him, "I'll follow you wherever you go." On the surface, you'd like to
think this is a good and encouraging passage. This is the ideal disciple, right?
Someone willing to quickly go wherever Jesus leads? Isn't this exactly what
you're looking for in a disciple when recruiting for your world-changing
movement?

Well, Jesus seems to think something deeper is going on. Look again at
his response:

> Foxes have holes, and birds of the air have nests, but the Son of Man
> has nowhere to lay his head.

Let's be honest, this feels kind of like an odd response to someone who just said they are willing to follow you wherever you go. What was Jesus trying to say here?

Well, it actually helps to look at this whole passage in its full context. If you rewind just a few verses earlier, look what Jesus says to the crowd:

> And he said to all, "If anyone would come after me, let him deny himself and take up his cross daily and follow me. For whoever would save his life will lose it, but whoever loses his life for my sake will save it. For what does it profit a man if he gains the whole world and loses or forfeits himself?" (Luke 9:23-25).

Here's another clue to help us understand what Jesus was trying to say to this first person. Fast-forward a couple chapters and listen to what Jesus says:

> Now great crowds accompanied him, and he turned and said to them, "If anyone comes to me and does not hate his own father and mother and wife and children and brothers and sisters, yes, and even his own life, he cannot be my disciple. Whoever does not bear his own cross and come after me cannot be my disciple. For which of you, desiring to build a tower, does not first sit down and count the cost, whether he has enough to complete it? Otherwise, when he has laid a foundation and is not able to finish, all who see it begin to mock him, saying, 'This man began to build and was not able to finish.' Or what king, going out to encounter another king in war, will not sit down first and deliberate whether he is able with ten thousand to meet him who comes against him with twenty thousand? And if not, while the other is yet a great way off, he sends a delegation and asks for terms of peace. So therefore, any one of you who does not renounce all that he has cannot be my disciple" (Luke 14:25-33).

Here's the point I think Jesus was trying to make to person number one:

It's going to cost a lot to follow me, and frankly, I'm not sure you've truly counted those costs yet.

When Jesus says that foxes have dens and birds have nests, he is implying that these animals have homes. And yet he says the Son of Man doesn't have a place to lay his head. He's homeless.

> **Are you quick to make big decisions without fully counting the cost of what you're getting into?**

Person number one was quick to follow Jesus, but he hadn't truly counted the cost. He was a runner. He ran to Jesus, but in his excitement, he missed the full ramifications of what this discipleship journey would cost him.

I'll be honest: I'm usually a runner when it comes to decision-making. I rarely take the time to sit down and count the cost. If you looked at my track record over the years, you would assume my life motto was "Ready! Fire! Aim!"

Let's pause right here for a second. As you reflect on your own life, can you relate to person number one in this passage? Are you quick to make big decisions without fully counting the cost of what you're getting into?

As you think about that, let's dive deeper into our passage.

> To another he said, "Follow me." But he said, "Lord, let me first go
> and bury my father."

Person two has an interesting story. He seems fully willing to follow Jesus, but before he goes all in as a disciple, he'd like to bury his dad.

It sounds like a reasonable request, honestly.

There's just one major problem: His dad was most likely still alive.

In the cultural context of this passage, it is likely that his father was still alive and living with him in the same house. When he says, "Let me first go and bury my father," he is likely saying, "Can I follow you after I finish taking care of my dad in his old age?"

And even if his dad had already passed away, he wouldn't be asking Jesus to attend a funeral that day that would take a couple hours. Instead, as a Jewish man, he would have spent days, if not weeks, going through the ceremonial burial process.

Again, that's if his father had already died, which is unlikely.

Either way, the point is this: Person two is willing to follow Jesus, just not right now. He has some things he needs to take care of ahead of time.

He is a waiter.

He's waiting to wrap up some loose ends before he can dive all in on the things God is calling him to. This is why Jesus responds with this:

> Leave the dead to bury their own dead. But as for you, go and proclaim the kingdom of God.

Let's look at the last person desiring to follow Jesus as one of his disciples.

> Yet another said, "I will follow you, Lord, but let me first say farewell to those at my home."

Just like person number two, we have someone willing to follow Jesus, but first...

We've learned by now that Jesus isn't looking for disciples who wait to be obedient. He is looking for followers who will go all in when he calls them to go all in.

> Jesus said to him, "No one who puts his hand to the plow and looks back is fit for the kingdom of God."

Person three was a waiter as well.

Jesus isn't looking for disciples who wait to be obedient. He is looking for followers who will go all in when he calls them to go all in.

Q&A MIXTAPE

Leila would be the first to admit that she's a waiter. In fact, we call her the tortoise of our family because of how slowly she makes decisions. You will never find her running toward anything (except maybe a coffee shop). When we are faced with a big decision as a family, she admits that she's willing to be obedient to the Lord's leading but most definitely has a few "but firsts…" she needs to take care of.

She's a waiter.

She waits to feel a full sense of peace. She waits for all the unknowns to become clear. She waits to see what others think about the situation.

I want you to stop and think about a decision that you're currently facing as a man or within your family. Are you being a runner that needs to slow down enough to count the cost and wait on the Lord?

> Wait for the Lord; be strong and take heart and wait for the Lord (Psalm 27:14 NIV).

Or has the Lord given clear direction to you, and yet you've still decided not to act in obedience? You're waiting on all your "but firsts" to be answered and taken care of before you move forward.

Regardless of where you find yourself on the runner and waiter spectrum, I want to share some practical tips you can use when faced with a big and difficult decision as a family. These are principles that have been passed down to me by others much wiser than I am. They are the same principles that Leila and I use time and time again when faced with any significant decision.

MAKING DECISIONS ALONE IS FOOLISH.
MAKING DECISIONS WITH TOO MANY PEOPLE IS CHAOTIC.

Limit your circle to two to five trusted friends who love Jesus and love you. Invite them to join you in prayer over the next several days, weeks, or months to seek wisdom from the Holy Spirit. Don't make any decisions alone, but also don't invite your entire Facebook or Instagram following to make decisions with you; that will likely lead to more confusion than wisdom.

DON'T BASE YOUR DECISION ON A LIST OF PROS AND CONS.

When we face major decisions, our first inclination is to make a list of every possible pro and con. While there is some wisdom in this strategy, it should never be the final determining factor for how the decision is made. As we study the Scriptures, we find loads of people who were called to be obedient to Jesus even when it didn't make sense to the rest of the world. In fact, I'd argue that most of the times God called people to obedience, they very rarely made sense to anyone else. Their "cons" list would have most definitely outnumbered their "pro" list, and yet God still called them to obey.

> As we study the Scriptures, we find loads of people who were called to be obedient to Jesus even when it didn't make sense to the rest of the world

I have made plenty of major decisions that did not look good on paper, or maybe even to the rest of the world (including becoming a foster parent). But through the leading of the Holy Spirit, the wisdom of his Word, and the counsel of those close to me, I moved forward anyway. Sure, you can make a pros and cons list to help add some data to the decision-making process, but ultimately, we must follow the Spirit's leading, even when it doesn't seem to quite make sense.

Waiting on the Lord is active, not passive.

Leila once told me that she heard a pastor say "It's hard for God to move a parked car" during one of his sermons. Now, while I believe God can do whatever he wants to do, regardless of what gear the car is parked in, I also believe there is some wisdom in this analogy. I think the point the pastor was trying to make was that you must be open, willing, and ready to act when God calls you to move. You may be in a season of life where God is calling you to wait on him and his direction. Perhaps a big decision is coming, but the timing is not right. You are doing your best not to run ahead of the Lord's direction, but you also don't know what to do in the meantime. If that's you, may I suggest that you shift the car from parked to "drive"?

> He may be calling you to obedience sooner than you realize.

Here's what I mean: Instead of eating Cheetos and watching Netflix as you wait on the Lord, use this time to prepare for what he might have for you. Preparing may look like beginning to chip away at debt so you can be more financially flexible. It may look like confessing sin or seeing a marriage counselor to make sure you don't bring that ongoing dysfunction or habit into this new season God will call you into. It may mean developing regular habits of prayer and study of God's Word personally or as a couple. The key here is to prepare for whatever God has for you so you can be quick to run to obedience and avoid making any "but first" excuses. Pack your bags, check your tires, fill the gas tank, and put the car into drive. He may be calling you to obedience sooner than you realize.

QUESTIONS TO CONSIDER

1. What decision are you currently facing as a man or as a family?

2. Who is on your "wise counsel" team? List three to five people who love you and love Jesus.

3. When it comes to decision-making, are you typically a "runner" or a "waiter"? What about your spouse?

4. What can you do in preparation to run toward obedience as you wait on the Lord?

5. What "but firsts" are keeping you from obeying Jesus quickly?

6. Are you united in your marriage when it comes to making this decision?

THE RIGHT HOOK

How Can I Deal with My Anger?

I have two friends who are successful fighters in the Ultimate Fighting Championship (UFC) league. They make their living by training, studying the martial arts, and competing against the best athletes in the world. They're absolute studs and by far the toughest guys I know.

Recently, our family had lunch with one of the fighters, Beniel Dariush, and his family. My ten-year-old son, Elijah, had a million questions for Beniel, but he couldn't wait more than five minutes after sitting down to ask his most pressing question:

"What's it like to get hit in the face?"

Beniel laughed. "Well, it's kind of interesting. When you're in the middle of a competition, and your adrenaline is pumping, you almost feel numb to it. The pain doesn't really sink in until after the fight is over."

"Wow!" Elijah said through a mouthful of chicken and rice.

Not long after our lunch together, Beniel had another competition that was televised worldwide. Our family ordered some pizzas and blocked the evening off on the calendar so we could watch and cheer on our friend.

After watching several of the preliminary fights featuring young up-and-coming athletes, I turned to Leila and said, "Honestly, I feel like I could do this."

She looked back at me with a blank stare on her face.

"What?" I asked, not able to read her body language. "Why are you looking at me like that?"

"You have pizza sauce all over your face, Jerrad. Why don't you work on fixing that, and then maybe we can talk about you taking a punch to the face."

"Come on, babe. Get serious. Look at Beniel! We're practically the same age, weight, and height. He's doing it just fine! I'm not trying to become a professional fighter, but maybe it would be good for me to join a gym and start learning some of this stuff!"

"I don't think so." I could tell she wasn't going to entertain my impractical idea.

"All right, fine." I turned to Elijah. "Hey, bud, why don't we get some boxing gloves and we'll practice at home."

"Yes! Please!" he begged.

I could feel Leila's eyes burning a hole into the back of my head.

Before I let her talk me out of it, I had my phone pulled out and was finishing my order for two sets of boxing gloves with free overnight delivery included.

The next day we started our amateur training via YouTube videos. We watched one or two short training clips until we both got bored.

"All right, bud. Let's just start practicing against each other. We'll go 50 percent effort. I don't want to hurt you—Mom would kill me."

And with that, we touched gloves like real fighters and began moving around the room with our hands up to protect our faces.

"Don't be afraid to hit me, buddy. These are big, soft gloves."

"I know, Dad. I'm just waiting for my shot."

I laughed and continued circling around the living room.

I wish I could say what happened next, but I truly don't remember. All I know is that out of nowhere, my eyes flashed and my ears started to ring.

"Dad! Dad! Whoa! I did it! That was awesome! What did it feel like?" Elijah was jumping up and down.

At this point I was on a knee, trying to figure out what was going on. Apparently my ten-year-old son had just knocked the cobwebs off my dusty brain with a right hook to my skull.

"Dad, you okay?" he asked, his excitement turning to a bit of nervousness.

"No. Yeah. I'm totally cool. I think your glove must have just poked me in the eye or something," I lied. "I'm going to go into the bathroom and see if you scratched my eye. I'm cool, though. Totally fine. Good job, son. I think that's probably good enough training for today. Let's pick this up again tomorrow."

I was trying my best to walk in a straight line back to my room.

Leila walked in a few minutes later to see me laying on our bedroom floor with a cold washcloth pressed against my forehead.

"What's wrong with you?" she asked. But I could tell she had already talked with Elijah and knew the answer.

"Ah, nothing. I'm fine. Just a little headache." I kept trying to play it off.

She laughed and walked out of the room.

Turns out, I'm not as physically fit as I thought I was.

DON'T CRY OVER SPILLED OATMEAL

I'm writing this portion of the book in my three-year-old daughter's bedroom. It's the only quiet place I could find in the house this morning. As I type this sentence, it's 10:48 a.m. Less than two hours ago, I was down in the kitchen trying to prepare her some oatmeal for breakfast when she had a complete meltdown.

"I wanted to pour the oatmeal in the bowl!" she shouted.

"Okay, I'm sorry, baby girl. I already poured it, so you'll just have to eat it now."

"No! I want to pour it in the bowl!"

"Please stop yelling—you're going to wake up your little sister." I tried to remain calm.

"*I. Want. To. Pour. The. Oatmeal!*" she screamed at the top of her lungs, and she pushed the bowl off the table and stomped her little feet on the hardwood floor.

At this point, my patience had reached its limit. "Fine!" I shouted back at her. "Pour your own oatmeal! But first you better clean up that mess and stop yelling before you get in a lot more trouble!"

I threw a new packet of oatmeal on the counter and stormed off, completely frustrated and emotionally out of control.

In those moments, it takes me about three minutes of removing myself from the situation before I feel like a complete idiot. It turns out, I'm not as emotionally fit as I thought I was.

Even now as I sit in her room and type this story, I feel a combination of frustration at myself for losing my cool and acting like a child myself along with sadness for the way I yelled at my baby girl. I'm looking at her little toys scattered around the room, and I feel like a scumbag.

> It turns out, I'm not as emotionally fit as I thought I was.

Even in this moment, I'm convicted by the Holy Spirit, knowing that I will need to go downstairs and make things right with her. I'm thankful that God parents my heart better than I often parent my own child's heart. He's always teaching me how to be a better father.

I'm thankful that God parents
my heart better than I often
parent my own child's heart.

PHYSICALLY FIT, EMOTIONALLY WEAK

One thing I often hear from the guys in our Dad Tired Family Leadership Program is that they struggle with showing emotion. During one of our recent trainings, I asked the guys, "On a scale from one to ten, how good do you feel about the way you present your emotions to your spouse?"

"I suck at it," one member blurted out immediately.

"Ha ha! Not really a number, but I think that sums up how many guys might feel," I responded.

I don't have any hard stats, but I would be willing to guess that most guys would admit to feeling emotionally stunted. That's no real surprise. What is surprising, however, is how we so often remove the emotion of anger when talking about our lack of ability to properly show how we're feeling.

> We may not be good at showing most of our emotions, but men seem to be fairly competent at displaying their emotion of anger.

Put frankly, we may not be good at showing most of our emotions, but men seem to be fairly competent at displaying their emotion of anger.

Just last week, I had a dad yelling at me from the sidelines as I coached a soccer team of ten-year-olds. I was able to keep my composure, but had I thrown a little gasoline on that emotional fire, I have no doubt it would have escalated to an embarrassing level for the both of us.

This is nothing new. You can search for videos online and easily find footage of dads fighting each other at their sons' Little League or Pop Warner games. Dads beating up referees. And dads punching each other in the face over road rage.

In fact, someone on my podcast recently shared a story of two dads who were fighting with each other while driving down the road with their families in two separate cars. The two dads each got out of their vehicles and shot each other. Apparently, they both died in front of their families.

When I searched for the story online, I literally found dozens of similar incidents that happened around the country within the last year. Dozens of men shoot each other, often in front of their families, because they have no control over their anger.

They are emotionally weak.

The truth is, most of us likely believe we're physically fit enough to take a punch, but we probably can't. And most of us would like to believe we are emotionally fit, but the reality is, many of us are pretty darn weak when it comes to controlling our anger.

> **Most of us would like to believe we are emotionally fit, but the reality is, many of us are pretty darn weak when it comes to controlling our anger.**

And as much as women generally have a reputation for being the emotional ones, it seems like the lack of emotional control in men is costing more lives.

These frequent and disturbing incidents of men losing control over their anger begins to beg the question, Why are men so angry?

When it comes to your own anger, how do you feel like you're doing at controlling that emotion?

For some guys, anger shows up through quick and snarky sarcastic comments when they are annoyed. For others, it presents itself through shouting, throwing something, or some kind of verbal outburst that they ultimately regret. Maybe for others, they turn inward and go silent, using

Left unchecked, the anger can turn violent or have emotional and relational ramifications that can't be undone.

Q&A MIXTAPE

their lack of words, emotions, or actions as a way to punish the person they are mad at.

Left unchecked, the anger can turn violent or have emotional and relational ramifications that can't be undone.

Where are you on that spectrum? When was the last time you felt really angry, and how did you respond?

Let's pause here for a minute and take the time to let the Scriptures teach, correct, rebuke, and train us for righteousness.[1] As you read these passages about anger, allow the Holy Spirit to speak to you. I often pray, "God, use your Word to show me where I am still unlike you. Train me up to be a disciple that looks more and more like you." Let's dive into the Word and allow him to do that for all of us.

- "Be angry and do not sin; do not let the sun go down on your anger, and give no opportunity to the devil. Let the thief no longer steal, but rather let him labor, doing honest work with his own hands, so that he may have something to share with anyone in need. Let no corrupting talk come out of your mouths, but only such as is good for building up, as fits the occasion, that it may give grace to those who hear. And do not grieve the Holy Spirit of God, by whom you were sealed for the day of redemption. Let all bitterness and wrath and anger and clamor and slander be put away from you, along with all malice" (Ephesians 4:26-31).

- "Know this, my beloved brothers: let every person be quick to hear, slow to speak, slow to anger; for the anger of man does not produce the righteousness of God. Therefore put away all

---

1. 2 Timothy 3:16.

What if our anger didn't have anything to do with what's going on *around* us but instead what's going on *within* us?

Q&A MIXTAPE

filthiness and rampant wickedness and receive with meekness
the implanted word, which is able to save your souls" (James
1:19-21).

- "Fools give full vent to their rage,
  but the wise bring calm in the end" (Proverbs 29:11 NIV).

- "Be not quick in your spirit to become angry,
  for anger lodges in the heart of fools" (Ecclesiastes 7:9).

- "You must put them all away: anger, wrath, malice, slander, and
  obscene talk from your mouth" (Colossians 3:8).

- "Refrain from anger, and forsake wrath!
  Fret not yourself; it tends only to evil" (Psalm 37:8).

- "What causes quarrels and what causes fights among you? Is it
  not this, that your passions are at war within you? You desire and
  do not have, so you murder. You covet and cannot obtain, so
  you fight and quarrel. You do not have, because you do not ask"
  (James 4:1-2).

I'll be honest, that last passage punched me in the spiritual gut: "Is it not
this, that your passions are at war within you?" The Holy Spirit used that
line to wreck me.

What if our anger didn't have anything to do with what's going on *around*
us but instead what's going on *within* us? What if you aren't mad at your
toddler for having a meltdown, your wife for disrespecting you, or that guy
who just cut you off on the freeway? What if your anger is in fact a volcano
from within that is simply using external situations as an excuse to erupt
into the world?

Truthfully, I didn't even realize I had a temper until I got married and had children. I had never seen myself lose my cool before then. It turns out, I have buttons that can be pushed that I didn't even know I had.

I've spent the last several years asking myself some questions that I'd like to now invite you to ask yourself too: *What's really behind my anger? Why does my anger seem to be larger than most situations call for? What's really going on?*

LOSS OF IDENTITY

I've shared before that I grew up without a father in the home. If that happens to be your story as well, you know the devastating impacts that can have on a young boy. Even as a grown man, I'm still discovering all the ways that being raised without a dad impacted who I am to this very day. One of the biggest consequences of a child being raised without a father is the subsequent lack of identity they struggle with throughout their life. When a child, especially a boy, does not constantly hear who they are from their father, they will likely spend a lifetime trying to discover their identity from the world around them.

> It turns out, I have buttons that can be pushed that I didn't even know I had.

A lack of secure identity in Christ results in grown men constantly asking the internal questions of *Am I good enough? Am I competent?* and *Do I have what it takes?* In an effort to answer those questions, you'll find men who are desperately looking to secure their identities through their work, accomplishments, bank accounts, hobbies, women, and anything else that will tell them, "You're doing a good job."

Dad, hear me on this: One of the greatest gifts you can give your children is a secure identity in Christ. One of your primary roles as the spiritual leader of your home is to consistently remind your children who they are in Christ—that they are loved, valued, and worthy, not based on anything they do, but simply because they are children of the Most High. Fail to do this, and you will likely find these same children grow into young men and women who are desperately searching the world around them to discover who they are.

It's in this unstable foundation of Christ-centered identity that the seeds of anger begin to grow.

Let me give you a practical example of how this plays out in the real world.

Remember my story about the dad who was yelling at me from across the field as I tried to coach a soccer team of ten-year-old boys?

> **One of the greatest gifts you can give your children is a secure identity in Christ.**

What if I consistently struggle with my identity, wondering, *Am I enough? Do I have what it takes?* These are often subtle questions, but they drive the behavior of most men. If these are the questions I am playing on a loop inside my brain, how am I supposed to respond when another man yells at me from across the field? He may be yelling, "Come on, Coach! Get it together!" But what I hear is, "You're not good enough. You don't know what you're doing. You don't have what it takes!"

These are the statements most men are internalizing from their bosses, their wives, and the world around them. And instead of believing we are who the Scriptures say we are in Christ, we desperately try to defend who we so badly want to be.

The next time you see two grown men arguing at a sporting event, swap out their words with these statements instead:

"You don't have what it takes!"

"Yes, I do!" *I think.*

"You're not good enough!"

"Yes, I am!" *I hope.*

"You're not worthy of doing this!"

"Yes, I am!" *Right?*

I wonder what would happen to our anger if we meditated on the truths of what God says about us instead of repeatedly questioning our identities. The truth is, it's a lot harder to let that dad on the other side of the field ruin my day by calling me a loser when I know that I've been chosen by the Creator of the universe.

> You are a chosen race, a royal priesthood, a holy nation, a people for his own possession, that you may proclaim the excellencies of him who called you out of darkness into his marvelous light (1 Peter 2:9).

Or that I'm deeply loved by God himself:

> In all these things we are more than conquerors through him who loved us (Romans 8:37).

Or that even though my own father failed to place identity on me, the heavenly Father chose me as his own son:

> See what kind of love the Father has given to us, that we should be called children of God; and so we are (1 John 3:1).

Brother, can I say something candidly to you? Secure men don't need to defend their identities. They aren't easily offended by the world around them. They have thick skin, not because they are tough or macho, but because they know exactly what their Father thinks about them.

And here's the thing: That kind of security doesn't come from a title on a business card, filling up a bank account, or adding more accomplishments to your life. That kind of security only comes from Christ. Everything else is sinking sand.

Insecure men are easily angered. Men who know who they are in Christ have a deep internal peace and security that cannot be shaken.

My buddy Jefferson Bethke once shared a benediction that he learned and now repeats with his own family. I absolutely love the way this simple benediction reminds us of who we are in Christ. I stole his idea, and now our family says it by memory almost every night before dinner. May I suggest that you also steal it and teach it to your children, allowing the truth of the benediction to sink deep into their hearts as they say it by memory? And as you listen to them speak these words out, close your eyes and remember that this same truth is also the gospel truth that Daddy needs so badly as well.

> Men who know who they are in Christ have a deep internal peace and security that cannot be shaken.

I'm not what I do.
I'm not what I have.
I'm not what people say about me.
I am the beloved of God.
It's who I am.
No one can take it from me.
I don't have to worry.
I don't have to hurry.
I can trust my friend Jesus.
And share his love with the world.[2]

LOSS OF PERSPECTIVE

Leila and I recently met up with a group of friends at the park to play a game of softball. One of the friends in our group was turning forty years

2. Bobby Schuller, "The Creed of the Beloved," in *You Are Beloved* (Nashville, TN: Nelson Books, 2018), 16.

old and thought it would be fun to celebrate by getting everyone together for some outside recreation. By the time the five couples arrived at the field, the temperature had dropped to just under forty degrees, and the rain was dumping so hard you could barely see into the outfield from home plate. Despite the less-than-ideal conditions, we threw on our jackets and ran onto the field. This was in Oregon, where you don't have the luxury of rescheduling because of the rain; otherwise, you'd be waiting indoors for nine months out of the year.

Our softball game was less of a game and more of an excuse for a bunch of adults to act like kids again. When was the last time you played at the park with your friends in the dumping rain—with no kids around? There were no strikeouts. No one was playing any proper positions. And we were barely keeping track of how many outs each team had.

After about thirty minutes of mainly just goofing off with a group of friends in the rain, I found myself standing on first base saying to myself, *Okay, Jerrad, the score is three to two. If you steal second base, you'll likely have a chance to get to home if Travis hits deep into left field, like he usually does. They don't have anyone over there to catch fly balls.*

I honestly don't know how long I was deep in my own strategic thoughts about the game, but at some point, I was abruptly interrupted when Leila yelled at me from the dugout.

"Jerrad! Jerrad!"

I snapped out of my trance and looked over at her.

"Whoa! You were deep into that thought. Welcome back," she said.

I laughed, trying to regain my focus.

"Sorry, babe. What's up?" I asked.

"I was just seeing if you wanted some marshmallows in your hot chocolate," she said with a sweet smile on her face.

For whatever reason, that question hit me like a two-by-four over the head. I had just spent the last several minutes deep in my own thoughts about how to win a softball game, while everyone else was thinking about how many marshmallows they wanted in their hot chocolate.

I'm embarrassed to say that I completely lost track of all reality. Here we were, playing the least competitive softball game in history. In the rain. In December. With no one around. And no one keeping score.

Not a single person in the entire world cared about what was happening in that game. Not even the people I was playing with. It was absolutely pointless in the grand scheme of things.

And yet I was on first base trying to strategize about how to score another point. I felt silly, to say the least.

Sometimes it helps to zoom out.

I keep thinking back to that story of the dads who got shot and lost their lives in front of their families because of road rage. I imagine if they could do it all over again, each would likely just brush off the guy who tried to cut him off on the freeway. I doubt they would admit that dying over their anger on the road meant more to them than their families did. When you zoom out, it seems absurd to think about. But in that moment, these men let their anger overrule them, and they lost all perspective of reality. They couldn't zoom out.

Sometimes it helps to zoom out.

The beautiful thing about zooming out is it allows you to see the end. You get to view the story in its full context. I'm not talking about zooming out by a couple hours or even a couple days (although that, too, would have been helpful). Even if each of these men had just thought to himself, *You know what, by the time dinner comes around, I won't even remember this jerk who cut me off,* that would have been helpful and probably would have saved his life.

But I'm talking about zooming out even further. Not hours. Not days. Not months. But years. Decades.

Pause with me and try to zoom out forty, fifty, or sixty years in your mind. Let's say, by God's grace, you've lived a long life. What does the end of your story look like?

For me, I imagine being surrounded by my kids, grandkids, and maybe even great-grandkids. I imagine my wife's wrinkly hand holding on to my old hand. I imagine looking into my kids' eyes with pride, as I see them passing on a godly legacy to their own children. I've watched how they've intentionally raised their own kids to know and love Jesus. I imagine thinking back on all the lives that God let me be part of. The men I tried to pour my life into so they could come to know Jesus in a deeper way. The kids, who are now adults, that we let into our home so they could feel safe when they had no other place to go. The kids I mentored through sports, or in the neighborhood, praying all the while that through our family they'd get a glimpse of how much God loves them. I imagine looking into the eyes of my wife and thanking God that he helped hold us together. That despite how challenging life and marriage can be, it was all worth it.

Listen, I know God can and will do whatever he wants to do with my life, but this is the kind of ending I desire for my own story. What does your ending look like?

> Therefore, since we are surrounded by so great a cloud of witnesses, let us also lay aside every weight, and sin which clings so closely, and let us run with endurance the race that is set before us, looking to Jesus, the founder and perfecter of our faith, who for the joy that was set before him endured the cross, despising the shame, and is seated at the right hand of the throne of God (Hebrews 12:1-2).

Not that I have already obtained all this, or have already arrived at my goal, but I press on to take hold of that for which Christ Jesus took hold of me. Brothers and sisters, I do not consider myself yet to have taken hold of it. But one thing I do: Forgetting what is behind and straining toward what is ahead, I press on toward the goal to win the prize for which God has called me heavenward in Christ Jesus (Philippians 3:12-14 NIV).

What's your finish line?

The other day I was brushing my teeth and looked into the mirror. It appeared that one of the hairs from my head had fallen off and landed on my ear. I took my free hand and went to brush the lone hair off my ear, only to find that it was attached.

"What in the world?!" I said out loud to an empty bathroom.

This wasn't a piece of hair that had fallen off my head; it was a hair growing from my ear! It turns out, as you get older, you lose hair in places you want it and grow hair in places you didn't even know were possible.

This disturbing discovery led me to lean in closer to the mirror, allowing me to study my whole face in more depth. What else was going on that I didn't know about?

As I looked at myself more closely than normal, I began to realize how much of my hair had turned gray. In fact, not just the hair on my head, but all throughout my beard too. The wrinkles in my forehead were looking more like canyons than they had the year before.

"Wow. I'm getting old." I said under my breath.

In that moment, I realized the weight of this verse in James:

> Come now, you who say, "Today or tomorrow we will go into such and such a town and spend a year there and trade and make a profit"—yet you do not know what tomorrow will bring. What is your life? For you are a mist that appears for a little time and then vanishes (James 4:13-14).

Brother, hear me in this moment: Life is a mist. These gray hairs and wrinkles on our faces are just outward signs that our bodies are rapidly moving toward death. The hairs on your head are literally dying as your body moves closer to its final days.

You and I will be gone very soon. Much sooner than we think or hope.

The most pressing question you can answer right now is, What does the end of your story look like? What does life look like when you zoom out decades from now?

Because here's the truth: If you don't have that figured out, you will start to convince yourself that what happens in the moment is the most important thing in the world. When you and I lose the perspective that we are simply sojourners in this short world, we find ourselves getting angry at really silly things.

> **You and I will be gone very soon. Much sooner than we think or hope.**

We blow up on our kids when they spill oatmeal on the kitchen floor.

We want to fight when a guy cuts us off on the freeway.

We lose our cool when someone disagrees with us online.

If we're not careful, we start to strategize about a softball game in front of an audience of no one.

Zoom out, man. What's the end goal here? When you have that down, you get a little less angry about the silly stuff.

It's just oatmeal. It's just a stranger on the freeway. It's just a softball game with your friends.

May we run toward the finish line set before us without getting distracted by the silly stuff.

QUESTIONS TO CONSIDER

1. Anger is rarely the first emotion. What do you think is really behind your anger? Is there something deeper going on?

2. Take a minute and write out your "finish line." As you zoom out, what are you hoping to see in your life forty or fifty years from now?

3. Do you feel like you are trying to prove yourself in order to secure your own identity? Who are you trying to convince that you're enough and that you have what it takes? Yourself, your boss, your dad, your wife? When do you find yourself doing that the most?

4. When do you find yourself getting angriest? Are there patterns? Try meditating on the truths of who Christ says you are next time you are in a situation that would normally cause you anger.

LAYERS ON LAYERS

Struggling with Pornography and Lust

I was twelve years old the first time I saw pornography.

I'm guessing I'll likely remember that day for the rest of my life. I didn't know it then, but that moment would significantly impact me for years to come.

I was having a sleepover at my friend Andrew's house. His parents had just fallen asleep, and we were playing James Bond 007 on the Nintendo 64.

"Hey, dude. You wanna see something funny?" Andrew interrupted our gaming to ask me.

"Heck ya!"

"Check this out." He set down his controller and walked over to the family computer. My family didn't have a computer at home, so my curiosity about this new fancy robot machine was high.

He sat down at the desk and hit the power button. The computer immediately started to make all kinds of weird sounds while it began the process of booting up. Five minutes later, and we were finally able to use the machine. He hovered his mouse over an icon with a blue lowercase "e" with what appeared to be a yellow halo circling around it.

"This is the internet. You can literally search for anything you want on here!" he said with a giant smile on his face.

"No way!" I was truly astonished.

"Watch this…" he said as he used his two pointer fingers to type.

He slowly pecked the letters "N A K E D G I R L S" on the keyboard.

My heart started to race. Before I could even figure out what was going on, about a dozen photos of nude women popped up on the screen.

My faced turned bright red and felt hot. I wouldn't have been able to describe it in the moment, but a huge wave of shame came crashing over me. I immediately thought of my mom and how disappointed she would be in me. And yet even with all these new emotions, the majority of which were not good, I still couldn't turn and look away.

"Isn't that awesome!" Andrew said, and then he suddenly hit the power button, causing the computer to jolt off.

"Wait! Why did you do that?" I asked, almost angrily.

"Do what?"

"Why did you turn off the computer?"

"If my mom or dad wakes up, they'll kill me."

"Come on, man. Don't be a wimp. Turn it back on," I insisted.

After going back and forth for a few minutes, I was able to convince Andrew to do one more search. My heart was nearly beating out of my chest, and yet I wanted to see more.

I had never seen a naked woman before. Honestly, I didn't even really know how sex worked at that time in my life. My dad wasn't around when I was growing up, and my mom never had "the talk" with me. I was her only boy, and the youngest; I can't imagine how awkward the thought of that must have been for her. And so she avoided it. I can't blame her.

I couldn't sleep that night.

Those images had been branded deeply into my brain. I played them on a loop repeatedly. I can't fully put into words what I was feeling. It was a combination of deep damning guilt, insatiable curiosity, and excitement.

I didn't know it then, but those feelings would become familiar companions of mine throughout my teenage years.

SWEET SINS

When was the first time you looked at pornography?

Notice how I didn't ask *if* you have ever looked at pornography but *when* you looked at it for the first time. I would be willing to bet that just about every single man who is holding this book has seen pornography at some point in his life.

Whenever I am invited to speak at a men's retreat, this topic inevitably comes up. And without fail, the room gets awkwardly quiet. I usually throw out this completely made-up statistic to lighten the mood a little:

"Did you know that 99 percent of men admit to struggling with porn at some level? And that the other 1 percent of men lie about it?"

The awkward silence is typically broken with some relieved chuckles throughout the room.

You might be feeling that same awkward tension right now just reading about this. What if your wife walks in and asks you what you're reading about? What if you're at a coffee shop and someone peeks over your shoulder?

I remember one time during youth group as a teenager, our youth pastor did breakout sessions to cover topics separately for boys and girls. The female youth leaders took all the girls into one room while he stayed back to have a separate talk with the boys.

"Guys, I want our group to be a safe place for you to share what you're struggling with."

Immediately my heart started to beat faster. I had looked at pornography several more times over the years since that first time at Andrew's house and had since been carrying around a heavy burden of guilt and shame. I was worried that this was about to be the moment where all my secrets were laid out for my friends to see.

Oh, crap, I thought to myself. *I'm going to be kicked out of this church tonight when they find out what I've been doing.* A thousand scenarios started to race through my head.

"I know this is probably hard for you guys, so I want to go first. I'm fully aware that a lot of you look to me as your role model, and I want you to know that I also have struggles too."

No way! I thought. *He's looked at pornography too?* For some reason, I felt relieved. Maybe I wouldn't be kicked out of the church if our youth pastor also had the same struggles I did.

"Listen, this is really hard for me to admit, but I've struggled with this for a long time." His voice got quieter.

I was at the edge of my seat. Never had I paid more attention during youth group than in this moment.

"I'll just come right out and say it: I'm very undisciplined when it comes to sweets. I've tried countless times to stop eating sweet treats, but I am addicted. It's something I've asked the Lord to help me with, but honestly, I feel like I have no self-control."

I sat in silence with what must have been the most confused look possible on my face.

You're kidding me, right? I thought to myself. *This is your big confession? That you eat too many sweets? Is this a joke?*

I didn't even know that eating too many sweets was a sin. I had eaten half a dozen donuts that morning before second period math class.

He rambled on for a few more minutes about all his deep "sweet" sins, but honestly, I stopped paying attention well before he finished. I remember feeling so lonely after that night. Not only was I disappointed that we didn't share the same struggles, but now I felt like I was even further down the broken path of guilt and shame. What's worse is that I left that night believing I was the only Christian walking down that road.

Can I let you in on a little secret?

That youth pastor, bless his heart, may have had a very real struggle with lack of self-control when it comes to desserts, but I can almost assure you that was not his greatest undertaking in life. He was young, and I truly believe he was doing his absolute best to disciple the young people of our church to become faithful followers of Jesus. I don't fault him in the least bit; and I mean that seriously. I'm hoping that many young guys walked away encouraged that night and felt the safety to share openly about their own shortcomings. But for me, it had the opposite effect. I left more determined than ever to keep my secrets in the dark because I was convinced that no other Christian, and certainly no church leader, could relate to my unique sins.

> **Keep the leaders hiding in their shame, and you can keep the flock crippled with their same sin.**

It turns out, I was wrong.

Fast-forward about twenty years, and I've now lost count of the number of pastors and church leaders who have been burdened by sexual sin for most of their lives. I have sat across the table from guys I respect tremendously, men of God who are leading massive movements for the kingdom, and yet have struggled with this topic.

In fact, I'm convinced that one of the main reasons your church likely doesn't talk about this subject more often is because many of the leaders have their own battles with the topic. It's a brilliant strategy from the evil one: Keep the leaders hiding in their shame, and you can keep the flock crippled with their same sin.

I'm not saying every leader looks at pornography. In fact, I think there are lots of godly men who are dedicated to purity on this subject. But I am saying that there are a lot more leaders who struggle with this than they'd like to admit.

My fear in sharing this with you is that you'll subconsciously use it as an excuse to overlook the seriousness of sexual sin.

Well geez, if my pastor struggles with pornography, then I'm probably not doing too bad, you might think to yourself. The bad news is, your pastor won't stand before God one day and give an account for your life. You will. God isn't grading on a sliding scale.

A COMFORTING SPECK

I want you to have the courage to pause for a minute for some self-reflection. How are you doing with sexual purity?

If you're like most dudes I know, right now you're likely trying to convince yourself that your secret habits aren't nearly as bad as you think they are.

I'm not addicted, you think to yourself. *I could stop whenever I wanted.*

If you relate to that last sentence, may I humbly ask, Why haven't you? Or even, Can you just spend the next ten days not looking at anything inappropriate?

How did that question make you feel? Did it make your chest tight? Did the thought of taking ten days off feel overwhelming? If so, you might be in deeper than most would like to admit.

Brother, the good news is, you're not alone. I spend my life working with Christian men, and just about every one of them would admit to struggling with pornography at some point in their lives.

The bad news? Just because most guys struggle doesn't make it any less destructive. This sin will destroy. It will destroy you, your marriage, and your family if left unchecked.

I love how the psalmist says it:

> Teach me, LORD, the way of your decrees,
>   that I may follow it to the end.
> Give me understanding, so that I may keep your law
>   and obey it with all my heart.
> Direct me in the path of your commands,
>   for there I find delight.
> Turn my heart toward your statutes
>   and not toward selfish gain.
> *Turn my eyes away from worthless things;*
>   *preserve my life according to your word* (Psalm 119:33-37 NIV).

Did you catch that last line? He connected the preservation of his life with his eyes looking at worthless things.

Do you take your sinful habits that seriously? In case that wasn't heavy enough, look at these verses from 1 Corinthians:

> Flee from sexual immorality. Every other sin a person commits is outside the body, but the sexually immoral person sins against his own body. Or do you not know that your body is a temple of the Holy Spirit within you, whom you have from God? You are not your own, for you were bought with a price. So glorify God in your body (1 Corinthians 6:18-20).

Listen, brother. I have good news for you. There is hope. But first you must let the weight of your sin sink in. Amazing grace is only amazing if you first recognize how badly you need it. Satan would love to convince you that you're doing okay because "everyone struggles with this." Don't buy into that twisted lie. Yes, others may be struggling, but their sin isn't directly impacting your relationship with Christ, your wife, your children, and the world around you.

Stop taking comfort that your brother also has a speck in his eye, and address the plank in your own. A massive surgery is needed in your own life; it doesn't matter how many other guys need that same surgery. All sins lead to death, and their sins won't feel as comforting when you're dead (spiritually, relationally, or otherwise).

> Amazing grace is only amazing if you first recognize how badly you need it.

Pause for a minute and let the weight of your sin sink in. Think back to the very first time you looked at pornography. What did you feel in that moment? How did it impact the rest of your life? How has it continued to impact you to this day?

ORGANIC GARDENS

Satan doesn't win. At least, he doesn't have to when it comes to this subject in your life.

I have a feeling that even though he knows he ultimately loses in the long run, he probably has a little bit of swag in his step as he reflects on all the lives he's destroyed on his way out.

Let's throw off that swag as we remind him, and ourselves, of the healing work that can be found in Jesus Christ. There is hope. This is not a secret that needs to go with you to the grave and leave a massive wake of destruction in the process.

In my personal experience, and in the experience of many men who are finding success when it comes to sexual purity, there seem to be three major keys to overcoming repeated habits of looking at pornography.

The first and most important is spiritual. Sexual sin is as much a spiritual issue as it is a physical issue. More pointedly, it's a worship issue. When humans turn to pornography, we are buying into the same lie that Adam and Eve bought into on the very first pages of Scripture: that there is something other than God that can deeply satisfy our souls.

> **Sexual sin is as much a spiritual issue as it is a physical issue.**

> Now the serpent was more crafty than any other beast of the field that the Lord God had made.

> He said to the woman, "Did God actually say, 'You shall not eat of any tree in the garden'?" And the woman said to the serpent, "We may eat of the fruit of the trees in the garden, but God said, 'You shall not eat of the fruit of the tree that is in the midst of the garden, neither shall you touch it, lest you die.'" But the serpent said to the woman, "You will not surely die. For God knows that when you eat of it your eyes will be opened, and you will be like God, knowing good and evil." So when the woman saw that the tree was good for food, and that it was a delight to the eyes, and that the tree was to be desired to make one wise, she took of its fruit and ate, and she also gave some to her husband who was with her, and he ate. Then the eyes of both were opened, and they knew that they were naked. And they sewed fig leaves together and made themselves loincloths (Genesis 3:1-7).

You know what's crazy about this passage? Satan used a piece of fruit to tempt Eve while she was standing in the middle of the greatest garden of all time. That truly is craftiness on another level. Eve could have turned away from Satan and grabbed the most organic, non-GMO, additive- or preservative-free, farm-to-table piece of fruit in the history of the world. But there was something about this particular piece of fruit that really caught her attention. Let's look at it again a little more closely:

> But the serpent said to the woman, "You will not surely die. For God knows that when you eat of it your eyes will be opened, and you will be like God, knowing good and evil" (Genesis 3:4-5).

Ahhh, there it is. It wasn't really the fruit that was tempting her, was it? She wasn't drawn toward a delicious piece of food; she was drawn toward something she thought she needed. She wanted something she thought you couldn't find in God. That was the temptation.

And that's likely the same temptation that you and I are falling into on this very day. Every time we see that image on the screen or in a movie or magazine, we are buying into the same lie that Eve bought into that day in the Garden: *This will bring my soul more satisfaction than Jesus can.*

The more you fall in love with Jesus and taste his goodness, the more convinced you will be that nothing else can compare.

But just like Eve, we are quickly met with the consequences of our decision: shame. Not only did it not bring our souls the kind of satisfaction they so badly desired; it actually made us feel worse than before.

Satan has been lying from day one, hasn't he?

Can I remind you of something? If you have decided to follow Jesus Christ as your Lord, you are standing in the middle of an amazing and plentiful garden. Satisfaction abounds. You can turn in any direction in the kingdom of God, and your soul will be satisfied.

> Oh, taste and see that the LORD is good!
> Blessed is the man who takes refuge in him! (Psalm 34:8).

The more you fall in love with Jesus and taste his goodness, the more convinced you will be that nothing else can compare.

Your worship was meant for him alone. He's the only one to whom you can give your devotion and be satisfied. The next time you are faced with the temptation to look at pornography, ask yourself, *Will this satisfy my soul more than Jesus can?*

SPIRITUAL DEFENSE LAYERS

Now, I'll be honest: I wish you could just ask yourself a good spiritual question every time you're tempted, and that would solve all your problems. Maybe for some, it can. But for most, this battle is multifaceted. It will require many layers of defense.

As you start to become more in tune with the spiritual battle happening around you, there are also some very practical measures you can take to guard your heart, eyes, and soul.

Step one is to ask yourself, *Will this satisfy my soul more than Jesus can?* That question alone will help cue your spirit to remind you that this battle is bigger than just a physical urge. But honestly, that question alone may not always be enough. If you're serious about winning this battle, you'll need more layers of defense.

At my house, I have several ways to protect my family from outside intruders. I have bright outdoor lights, a sign in my yard that reminds the bad guys that we have a security system, heavy-duty dead bolts, firearms, and many other tools. The lights alone may not be enough, but in combination with all the other measures, I am putting up a much larger barrier to entry for bad guys who try to break into my home.

> If you're serious about winning this battle, you'll need more layers of defense.

Think of each of these strategies as tools to keep the darkness of evil away from your spiritual home.

One of your layers should include limited access to the online world without some level of accountability. If you let a child play unattended with fire long enough, eventually he will burn himself. And if you give a sinful man unlimited access to a dark world, eventually he'll willingly open the door to let the darkness walk right in.

Limited access to the online world can come in various forms. As you evaluate your own struggle with pornography, you'll have to decide which tools work best for you. This may mean not having a smartphone with internet access. I know that sounds old school, but Jesus was even more extreme than I am:

> If your right hand causes you to sin, cut it off and throw it away. For it is better that you lose one of your members than that your whole body go into hell (Matthew 5:30).

I'll let you apply that verse to your own life, but personally, I'd rather take the phone with no internet.

If a smartphone is a must for you, then consider downloading filters that will force you to pause before diving into that next impulse. Software services like CovenantEyes or Accountable2You work great, but there are many others out there.

Limited access may also mean things like allowing your spouse to have complete access to your phone, computer, and passwords. It may mean always being with someone when you're on a computer or watching television or movies.

At the end of the day, this battle against pornography will require much more than an accountability software or some rules around when you can or can't be on the internet. However, if you're serious about protecting your spiritual home, don't skip over this essential layer of spiritual security.

TOGETHER IN THE TRENCHES

This last one is one of the most important, and likely the hardest: You need to tell someone about your struggles.

If you're serious about winning this battle and becoming the spiritual leader that your family longs for you to be, you can't do this alone. You will need at least one or two guys who are in the trenches with you. You've got to confess your sins to one another regularly and pray for one another.

> Confess your sins to one another and pray for one another, that you may be healed. The prayer of a righteous person has great power as it is working (James 5:16).

You can recognize this battle with pornography is a spiritual battle until you're blue in the face. You can set up every accountability software on the planet. But this is where the real healing comes in—when two brothers sit across from each other, confess their sins, and pray for each other.

I have yet to meet a man who has found success in this area that hasn't taken this verse and command seriously. In other words, I have yet to meet a man who beat this battle alone.

Remember when I told you that just about every guy I know admits to struggling with pornography in some shape or form? That's good news—not because it allows you to continue with your sin knowing you're not alone, but because it allows you to confess your sins freely to another brother, knowing that he likely has struggled in the same way you are.

You need to tell someone about your struggles.

If you truly want to find success when it comes to sexual purity, you are going to need to find a brother who will walk with you in this. And my guess

If you're serious about winning this battle and becoming the spiritual leader that your family longs for you to be, you can't do this alone.

Q&A MIXTAPE

would be, he'll be just as glad to have someone in his corner as you will be to have him in yours.

Before we end this chapter, I'd like to give one very important caveat. The strategies I mentioned above come from my own experience and the experiences of many men that I've personally worked with. But I am fully aware that my experiences are not exhaustive. You may be struggling with very deep trauma, addiction, or a combination of the two. I am not a counselor, a doctor, or a psychiatrist, and I would be doing you a disservice by trying to convince you that all you need to do is take my advice and you'll be healed. I'm convinced that many of these steps will help propel you in the right direction spiritually, but if you believe there is something deeper going on, I implore you to meet with your pastor or a licensed Christian counselor to discuss your unique situation.

> **If you truly want to find success when it comes to sexual purity, you are going to need to find a brother who will walk with you in this.**

QUESTIONS TO CONSIDER

1. What emotions did you feel as you read this chapter? Did you sense any feelings of guilt or shame trying to creep up? How did you feel by the end of the chapter? Do you feel a sense of hope?

2. When you think about confessing your sins regularly to another brother, is there someone that comes to mind? Would you be willing to reach out to him in the next forty-eight hours to try to meet?

3. When do you feel most susceptible to looking at pornography? Are there any layers of defense that might help next time you're in that moment? What would they be?

4. Do you know anyone personally who has found success in this area? Would you be willing to sit down with them and ask them to share how they were able to remain pure?

HOW CAN I MANAGE TECHNOLOGY IN OUR HOME?

Last week I was having lunch with a friend whom I respect a ton. He has children who are about ten years older than mine, and I truly look up to the way he lives his life as a godly father. He works hard, loves his wife well, and is raising children who know and love the Lord. So I said, "Man, I look up to you a ton. If you were my age and could go back ten years, what would you change about the way you parented your kids?"

He sat quietly for a minute, as I could tell he wanted to give me a truly thoughtful and helpful answer.

"I would have never given them smartphones or let them on social media. I thought we had done enough when they were young children to prepare them for the digital world, but honestly, I would have waited as long as possible."

His answer surprised me, to be honest. He is one of the most godly and wisest men I know. I think I was expecting some long answer with tons of biblical references. And yet as he reflected on his years of parenting, his one regret had to do with technology.

I've been thinking about his answer for the past few days.

Statistically, I'm about halfway through my life expectancy, if I'm lucky enough to live a long life. When I reflect on my life, and more specifically my relationship with God, the most beautiful and profound moments had nothing to do with anything technological. In fact, quite the opposite. Every time I seemed to experience God in new and profound ways, I was removed from technology. These experiences, moments of clarity, and monumental discipleship moments almost always happened outside, looking at a sunset, on a mountain, around a fire, at the shores of an ocean, or at a dinner table. It was in these slow, unhurried, and undistracted moments that God drew my heart closer to his.

What about you? When you think back on all the times you've truly experienced God working in your life, what was going on? Where were you? Was there a phone, TV, or screen around?

> I can't blame my wickedness on technology, but it certainly has been used to speed up and magnify the desires of my flesh.

Let me take it one step further. Not only could I not think of a time where technology pushed me toward Jesus in significant ways, but more often than not, technology was actually being used to push my heart further away from things of the kingdom.

Technology is often the highway my flesh travels on to experience anger toward others, to lust after people and things I don't have, and to ultimately distract my heart from finding true rest and satisfaction in Christ alone. I can't blame my wickedness on technology, but it certainly has been used to speed up and magnify the desires of my flesh.

I know I sound like an old man. Maybe I'm just caught in the nostalgia of my youth. But I'd like to believe there are still moments of tech-free life where God can be found. And I want my children to experience that.

I've decided that I'm going to take the advice of my good friend, and I'm inviting you to as well. My kids don't have phones, and they won't anytime soon. I won't be signing them up for any social media accounts. I'm sure they'll hate me for it at some point, but for now, my goal is to build as many quiet, unhurried, and undistracted family moments as possible. Moments where the voice of God has the space to speak to their growing hearts and to show off his glory in new ways.

Our family often eats dinner around a candle. We try to go outside for a walk as often as the weather allows. We've traded video games for board games and TV screens for books.

It's not the technology that I'm mostly afraid of. I believe God can use anything to see his kingdom come on earth as it is in heaven. I'm writing this book on a fancy technological piece of equipment, and I run my entire ministry online. God most certainly uses technology for his glory.

I guess what I'm most worried about is the lack of silence. The constant distractions. The training of my child's young brain and heart to never be able to recognize the voice of God because there is too much noise.

Here's a challenge I recently accepted, and I invite you to try it too: Walk through your home and count every piece of technology you own that adds to the noise of your family's life. What would it look like if you cut that number in half and replaced them with something quieter for the soul? You could trade your smart speaker for a guitar or piano. Instead of streaming a song, try singing one together instead.

> **As spiritual leaders, we must train our children to be comfortable with simplicity and silence.**

Replace a TV or game console with a few board games. Replace a light with some candles.

As spiritual leaders, we must train our children to be comfortable with simplicity and silence because it's often in the simple and silent moments that God's presence shapes our hearts in the most profound ways.

POCKET PREACHERS

Do I Really Need to Go to Church?

A few months ago, I was back in California visiting my family. During one of the days of our trip, I decided to load my kids up in the rental car and give them a tour of the city I grew up in. I think I was way more excited about this little adventure than they were, but I promised to end our trip with ice cream, so they obliged.

We spent the next hour or so weaving in and out of the old streets that were once so familiar to me. As we did, floods of memories started to rush through my mind.

"Look, guys! That's the house where I grew up!" I said as I pulled the car over to the side of the road.

I started to share details about the neighbors I grew up playing with, my first job as the local paperboy, and where I got in my first fight as a sixth grader. They had no idea what a paperboy was, but their ears perked up when I mentioned that Daddy once got in a fight. Suddenly they wanted to know every detail of the story.

We continued our little drive and found the church my grandma had attended as a young woman. Honestly, I almost passed right by the building because it was hardly recognizable.

"Old Town Brewery," a giant sign read on the front of the building.

What in the world? I thought. *Where did the church go?*

I rolled down my window and called the attention of a young couple who were making their way to the entrance.

"Hey, guys. Sorry to bother you…just wondering if this is still a church?"

"Ummm, I don't think so," the young tattooed and bearded guy said with a confused look on his face. "But it's definitely a great place to try out some local beers."

"Oh, okay. Thanks, man," I said, rolling up my window.

"Not quite the spirits I remember this building being filled with," I said to my kids in the back seat. My dad joke went right over their heads.

When I returned to my family's house, I pulled out the computer to do some research. It turns out that old church had been turned into a local brewery almost ten years earlier. Before closing, it had lasted nearly a hundred years as a place of worship before church attendance had dropped to an unsustainable rate.

I felt a weird mix of emotions come over me as I continued to read.

That church was where my grandma met Jesus for the first time. It's where she would eventually be discipled in the faith and grow in her knowledge and understanding of what it meant to be a follower of Christ. It's where she took my mom to Sunday school and where she would eventually believe the good news of the gospel as well. God used that little church to capture the heart of my grandma and eventually my mother. As a result, I was introduced to the saving work of Jesus and am now trying my best to raise my own children to know and love God.

In short, generations of kingdom work have grown from the seeds that were planted in that little church. And now, it was a brewery.

CHURCH IN THE POCKET

The closing of my grandma's church is sad, but honestly, it isn't rare.

One recent study shows that there are more churches closing their doors due to attendance shortages than are being planted in the United States.[1] But you don't need to read a study to know that. Just drive around your local town. There may be a church on every corner, but how is attendance? Across the board, more and more churches are having to shut their doors because their congregants have stopped showing up.

I'm not a researcher or expert in this data, but I remember personally seeing this trend among my own peers around 2008. What happened in 2008? Well, the iPhone had just been released into the world a year earlier and was completely flipping everyone's reality on its head. The power of the internet was sitting in people's pockets.

You no longer needed to rent movies at Blockbuster because you could now stream them directly from your handheld device. Have a stockpile of CDs you've been collecting in your car? You can toss those out too because now every song in the world was at your fingertips.

Everything was immediately accessible. Including church.

Everything was immediately accessible. Including church.

I remember the first time my friend shared a sermon with me that he had listened to on YouTube. The preacher was full of charisma and was sharing perspectives on passages of Scripture that I had never heard before. My mind was blown. I had never heard that kind of preaching, especially not in our little town.

---

1. Aaron Earls, "Protestant Church Closures Outpace Openings in U.S.," Lifeway Research, May 25, 2021, https://lifewayresearch.com/2021/05/25/protestant-church-closures-outpace-openings-in-u-s/.

The craziest part to me was that I didn't need to fly to a conference or buy the DVD to watch it later. I could watch any sermon I wanted, on demand. And I did. I binge-watched countless messages during the week. I would listen as I worked or did chores around the house. I consumed more sermons within a matter of months than I probably had in my entire lifetime up until that point.

During that time, I remember going to church on Sunday mornings and subconsciously starting to compare the quality of the messages I was watching online to the message I was listening to from my local pastor. Sure, it was good and had a few little nuggets of wisdom, but it didn't even come close to comparing to the thought-provoking messages I had been binge-listening to all week long on my phone.

> As a young adult, I started to ask myself the same question that many of my friends began to ask: *Why do I even need to go to church?*

And then there was the worship.

My phone was now filled with Christian bands, solo artists, and songs playing the kind of music that would never be found in my church. They made our worship team look like a third-grade orchestra.

As a young adult, I started to ask myself the same question that many of my friends began to ask: *Why do I even need to go to church?* Truthfully, I could find biblically sound messages and worship directly on my phone anytime during the week. Not only that, but because of the invention of this new technology, I could even talk to my friends and find "community" online in a way that had never been possible before.

Now, I want to pause right here because your heart rates might be increasing. These words might be making you extremely uncomfortable.

Come on, Jerrad! You're nearly shouting at the pages. *Sure, you can find messages and worship online, but nothing compares to the local church!*

And I don't disagree with you. But we can't keep our heads in the sand either. Look around you. Churches are closing by the dozens. Church attendance is dropping faster than we can keep up with nationwide, especially among young people. If this trend continues, our towns will be filled with more Old Town Breweries than places of worship.

Like it or not, many young people believe that the faith of their parents is irrelevant altogether. And even for those not abandoning their faith completely, they are now filling their spiritual tank with messages, music, and community online, not in a building.

I know that makes us feel all kinds of emotions, but those emotions do not change the facts. So with those facts in mind, we must start asking ourselves some hard questions.

I'm fully aware that you may be a faithful church attender. You were raised in church, have attended church all your life, and are committed to raising your own children in the local church as well. If that's you, you should be proud. You're carrying on a godly legacy that is worthwhile. I would just ask you to consider thinking through one thing as the spiritual leader of your home: The day will inevitably come when your children or grandchildren will question the tradition that has always been part of your family. As our culture continues to move further away from any Christian values, they will eventually ask, "Why do we even need to go to church?"

Answering "Because we just do!" or "Because that's what our family does and has always done" may work while your children are young, but it will likely not hold up as they grow older. They need more than a simple "Because I said so."

Or you may be asking that same question yourself. Maybe you've been hurt by the church or a church leader. Maybe you just can't find a good church that checks all the boxes your family is looking for in a Christian community. Or maybe your family schedule is just so busy you can't imagine filling up another day of the week; you'd much rather sleep in and watch a football game than set your alarm on a weekend.

I'll just listen to the podcast later, you think.

Whether you're preparing to give a thoughtful answer to your teenage child or are asking the question personally, let's take a deeper look. Here are a few questions I'd ask you to consider.

WHAT IS THE CHURCH MISSING IF YOU'RE NOT THERE?

I wish I had a dollar for every time I heard these words: "My family and I are just looking for a good church with solid biblical teaching, good worship, and a great program for the kids."

> What if instead of going to a church to find all the ways it can serve your family, you went with eyes to see how your family can contribute to the larger body of Christ?

None of those things are wrong. I want your family to be part of a local church with sound biblical theology, engaging corporate worship, and a children's program that helps equip you to raise young disciples. But may I just suggest that we change our premise when trying to find a church with these qualifications?

The truth is, as we've already discussed, if all you're looking for is good teaching, great music, and a way to keep your kids active, you don't really need a church to do that. Your phone and the local kids' karate gym can check all those things off your list.

What if instead of going to a church to find

all the ways it can serve your family, you went with eyes to see how your family can contribute to the larger body of Christ?

> Just as the body is one and has many members, and all the members of the body, though many, are one body, so it is with Christ. For in one Spirit we were all baptized into one body—Jews or Greeks, slaves or free—and all were made to drink of one Spirit.

> For the body does not consist of one member but of many. If the foot should say, "Because I am not a hand, I do not belong to the body," that would not make it any less a part of the body. And if the ear should say, "Because I am not an eye, I do not belong to the body," that would not make it any less a part of the body. If the whole body were an eye, where would be the sense of hearing? If the whole body were an ear, where would be the sense of smell? But as it is, God arranged the members in the body, each one of them, as he chose. If all were a single member, where would the body be? As it is, there are many parts, yet one body.

> The eye cannot say to the hand, "I have no need of you," nor again the head to the feet, "I have no need of you." On the contrary, the parts of the body that seem to be weaker are indispensable, and on those parts of the body that we think less honorable we bestow the greater honor, and our unpresentable parts are treated with greater modesty, which our more presentable parts do not require. But God has so composed the body, giving greater honor to the part that lacked it, that there may be no division in the body, but that the members may have the same care for one another. If one member suffers, all suffer together; if one member is honored, all rejoice together.

> Now you are the body of Christ and individually members of it (1 Corinthians 12:12-27).

I spent more than a decade working on the staffs of local churches, and in my experience, very rarely did someone new walk through the doors asking, "What part of this body of Christ is missing or lacking? We'd like to try to help." Instead, I heard phrases like these more often: "I don't like the way they preach," or "They always play songs that I don't know."

> Brother, you need the local church, most definitely. But don't be fooled. The local church needs you too.

Brother, you need the local church, most definitely. But don't be fooled. The local church needs you too. It needs your family. There may be a local church in your neighborhood that's like a hand missing some fingers because you've convinced yourself that you can just find church online.

Maybe the next time your child asks why they need to go to church, instead of saying "Because I said so" or "That's what we do," you could remind them that the body of Christ is incomplete without them. Your family is uniquely designed to play a significant role in the kingdom of God at your local church.

The local church needs you to show up as much as a body needs legs to walk. They don't just need more greeters, coffee makers, and tithers. They need dads to mentor young kids. They need families to come alongside the widow. They need men to model for the young guys what it looks like practically to love your wife the way Christ loves his church. They need your daughter's perspective on the world and your son's courage to boldly proclaim his faith.

There is a local church in your neighborhood missing out on a significant part of the body of Christ because you're not there.

WHO WILL GUIDE YOU WHEN YOU GO ASTRAY?

Early on in marriage, Leila and I went through a terrible season. Like, really bad.

Your family is uniquely designed to play a significant role in the kingdom of God at your local church.

Q&A MIXTAPE

We both secretly were planning the divorce in our heads and trying to figure out the logistics of how we would handle raising the kids in separate homes.

At the time, I was acting completely rebellious and immature. I was deep in my own sin, and as a result, I pulled away relationally from my wife, my kids, and our group of friends. The last place I wanted to be was near people who knew me, and especially around Christians. It's amazing how much effort we will put in to avoid the light when we're living in darkness.

> There is a local church in your neighborhood missing out on a significant part of the body of Christ because you're not there.

One of the older guys from our church kept calling my phone repeatedly. He was not only an elder at our church but also a close friend. I knew he loved me and my family, but I just couldn't get myself to answer the phone.

Finally, I relented.

"Hey, man. How are you doing, bro?" he gently asked.

I immediately broke down. I had been trying to build up a tough exterior to the outside world, but the moment I cracked the door open to vulnerability, my fortress came crumbling down.

"I'm not good, man. I don't know what's going on with me, but I need help," I said through tears.

"Come over. Let's figure this out together."

I spent the next several months slowly making my way back into my church community. I wish I could say they just rubbed my back and told me everything was going to be okay. Admittedly, there was some of that, but there were also some really hard conversations. The men of the church sat with me, looked me directly in the eyes, and told me some really hard things. Some of the hardest things I've ever heard.

And yet in the midst of hearing these hard things, I felt loved. It reminded me of this verse:

> For the moment all discipline seems painful rather than pleasant, but later it yields the peaceful fruit of righteousness to those who have been trained by it (Hebrews 12:11).

Their discipline was definitely painful. But you know what happened? As a result of having guys around me who loved me enough to tell me some really hard things, I am now able to see the "peaceful fruit of righteousness."

As I write these words from my kitchen table, I'm looking around at my two oldest kids who are laughing while playing a card game with each other. My wife is nursing our baby girl on the couch. And our three-year-old is playing with her dolls on the floor. Is there better fruit than that?

That's the result of healthy church discipline. And you know what? You can't get that on your phone.

If you're serious about leading your family well, you must be humble enough to surround yourself with some people who love you enough to call you out on your sin.

> **If you're serious about leading your family well, you must be humble enough to surround yourself with some people who love you enough to call you out on your sin.**

> Whoever loves discipline loves knowledge, but he who hates reproof is stupid (Proverbs 12:1).

I don't want to be a stupid leader. I'm guessing you probably don't either. These are harsh words (from Scripture, not from me). But honestly, they are true. It would be stupid of us to try to lead our families while not submitting ourselves to others. You will fall off track. It's not a matter of if, but when. May we be men who are brave enough to love discipline when that time comes.

Why do we go to church? Not because we have to, but because we know ourselves well enough to know that we are prone to wander away from the things of God. And when that time comes, we want to be the kind of men who willingly submit ourselves to godly accountability; the kind that is impossible to find on a phone.

WHO WILL REMIND YOU THAT THIS STORY IS BIGGER THAN YOU?

This past weekend I was standing in our church auditorium, singing along with the rest of the congregation while holding our one-year-old in my arms. My wife and other children were standing next to me, singing along as well. As I looked around the dimly lit room, I saw an elderly couple standing about fifteen rows away from our family. They were holding hands, and the woman was lifting her other arm as she worshipped. A young couple was to my left, trying to settle into their seats with their brand-new infant. On stage was a teenage boy with a big smile on his face as he strummed his electric guitar in rhythm with the rest of the worship team.

Generations of people filling one room, singing to one God. It happens every week in our church, but in this moment, the weight of it really struck me. It was powerful.

You know what's amazing about being in a room full of other believers? You tend to feel a little smaller. As your voice gets lost within the crowd of voices, you start to recognize that there is something bigger going on around you. That maybe this whole story of humanity is bigger than you and bigger than your little family.

Let's be honest: We all get caught up in the notion that the whole world revolves around us. Many of us spend our week putting our heads down and moving on to the next thing with determination. As young dads, we can get lost in the chaos of just trying to provide for our family, making sure food is on the table, and doing our best to get our kids to sleep through the night.

> **This story of God redeeming all of humanity back to himself is big. Really big.**

There's something about being in a room full of people that forces you to lift your head up a little so that you can see the world around you. You start to think, *Maybe this story isn't just about me and my family. Maybe God is doing something really big around the whole world.*

And he is.

God is chasing you down with his love. He's chasing down your wife and your kids with his love. But he's also chasing down that elderly couple to your right. And that young couple to your left. He's chasing down that teenage boy as he sits in his room and tries to teach himself a few more chords on the guitar.

This story of God redeeming all of humanity back to himself is big. Really big.

Why do we go to church? Because we don't want to forget that our family is playing a small role in a much bigger story. We don't neglect gathering together as believers because we want to be reminded that God has been working for generations before us.[2] And he'll be working for generations long after we are gone.

Sure, my phone may be able to pull up some awesome sermons from a

---

2. Hebrews 10:24-25.

Why do we go to church?
Because we don't want to forget
that our family is playing a small
role in a much bigger story.

Q&A MIXTAPE

preacher in a faraway land. I may be able to stream the latest worship album from today's best worship bands. But I don't get to see that elderly couple to my right worshipping their Savior. I don't get to watch the young couple to my left as they learn what it means to parent their child's heart the same way God is parenting theirs. I miss out on watching that teenage boy grow in his discipleship journey.

You can get great sermons and worship on your phone, but that'll just keep your head down. Being part of local churches allows us to lift our eyes up long enough to see that the story is not about us. It's way bigger. And that my friends, is really good news.

QUESTIONS TO CONSIDER

1. As you read this chapter and reflect on your own life, do you feel like you have approached the church as somewhere to serve or somewhere to be served?

2. What are your current feelings toward being part of the local church? What do you think shaped your thoughts toward the local church?

3. If your kids were to ask you to explain why they need to be part of the local church, what would your answer be?

4. What unique qualities, gifts, and characteristics does your family possess that would add value to your local church?

FINAL THOUGHTS

I'm always amazed by the guys who make it to the end of a book. Honestly, I've only done that a few times in my life. I can't thank you enough for taking the time to read it, and I sincerely pray that it was helpful for you on your journey of leading your family well.

Admittedly, we were only able to scratch the surface on many of these topics. I know there are also many other pressing questions we were never able to address.

If you're longing for more resources on how to lead your family well, we would love for you to take a deep dive into our Dad Tired community. We have books, meetups, conferences, videos, training programs, and weekly podcasts all dedicated to helping equip you to lead your family well. You don't have to do this spiritual thing alone; there are plenty of guys who would love to stumble their way forward alongside of you.

This life is short, brother. Set aside the distractions and run the race that has been set before you.

I love you. Thank you for reading.
Jerrad

DO YOU WANT TO BE A SPIRITUAL LEADER?
START HERE

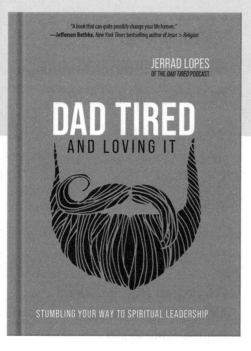

Have the day-to-day realities of being a dad and husband left you frustrated or just plain worn out?

YOU'RE NOT ALONE.

Jerrad Lopes, host of the popular *Dad Tired* podcast, helps you understand the bigger picture of God's purpose for you in your marriage and how the good news of Jesus makes it possible for you to love and lead your family without fear and discouragement.

ARE YOU TIRED OF TRYING ...AND FAILING?

"If you are a man seeking to fall more in love with Jesus and help your family do the same, this book is for you!"
—**David Robbins,** President and CEO, FamilyLife

JERRAD LOPES
OF THE *DAD TIRED* PODCAST

STOP BEHAVING

A GOSPEL-CENTERED DEVOTIONAL FOR CHANGE THAT LASTS

BEATING AN ADDICTION.

BEING A BETTER HUSBAND OR DAD.

FOLLOWING GOD MORE CLOSELY.

Whatever your challenge is, simply "trying harder" to change your behavior can create a cycle of failure and frustration, when what you really need is more of Jesus.

IT'S TIME TO STOP "BEHAVING" AND START LETTING HIM CHANGE YOUR HEART.

Available wherever books are sold. To learn more about *Stop Behaving* and other resources for dads, **VISIT » DADTIRED.COM.**

ENGAGE WITH GOD'S WORD

Jerrad Lopes, host of the *Dad Tired* podcast, introduces you to the basics of reading and reflecting on God's Word and gives advice on how to get the most out of your time with God.

Enhance your experience with the Bible today and learn how to better love and lead your family.

Sign up for the latest news from Dad Tired and get a free eBook with ten practical ways to point your family toward Jesus. To sign up and get your eBook, **GO TO » DADTIRED.COM/FREEBOOK.**

To learn more about Harvest House books and
to read sample chapters, visit our website:

www.harvesthousepublishers.com

HARVEST HOUSE PUBLISHERS
EUGENE, OREGON